Hidden in Plain Sight

Unearthing and Earthing the Psalms

— JOHN HOLDSWORTH —

Sacristy Press

Sacristy Press
PO Box 612, Durham, DH1 9HT

www.sacristy.co.uk

First published in 2023 by Sacristy Press, Durham

Sacristy Limited, registered in England & Wales, number 7565667

British Library Cataloguing-in-Publication Data
A catalogue record for the book is available from the British Library

ISBN 978-1-78959-319-8

Contents

Abbreviations

ESV	English Standard Version
CCP	Celebrating Common Prayer
NRSVUE	New Revised Standard Version, Updated Edition
REB	Revised English Bible

Introduction

On the face of it, there seems little in common between the Old Testament book of Psalms and the 2023 Eurovision Song Contest. But perhaps they have more in common than we suspect. Eurovision 2023 was hosted by Ukraine but staged in Liverpool. The previous year Ukraine's song had won, but even then the war with Russia was raging, and things were even worse in 2023, making it impossible to stage the contest there. Here were new songs, competitive songs, sung against the background of war, grief and loss but, despite everything, being sung in defiance, and against a groundswell of feeling that the brutality unleashed by Putin's Russia should not be allowed to have the last word. Surely there would be a time when justice would prevail, peace would come, and singing could be heard again in Kyiv.

The book of Psalms probably reached its final form sometime after the Exile, according to many scholars in the third century BCE. The editing activity was complemented by that of the scholars and theologians who were collecting the traditions that would go to make up the Torah and the Prophets. Imagine yourself as a compiler at this point. You are aware of the traditions which speak of how Israel was formed, and of the relationship with God which gave it its special character. You are aware that King David ruled over a united kingdom around 1000 BCE, but that soon after his time the kingdom was divided, and most of what you know about what happened then is from sources originating from Judah, the relatively tiny area around Jerusalem, which has Jerusalem as its capital. You are aware of the more recent catastrophe which overtook Judah when Jerusalem was ransacked by the Babylonians and the people taken into exile in Babylon in 597 and 587 BCE.

But even then, that was hundreds of years ago. You are probably a descendant of one of the families that returned from exile and tried to make the best of things by rebuilding the temple and restoring the city. Your job at present is to put together a hymnbook for use primarily in that temple. However, far from restoring Jerusalem's former glory, for hundreds of years since people returned in the late sixth century, Judah has been ruled by various colonial powers, some of which have been careless of the local culture and religion. The Persians overcame the Babylonians. The Greeks overcame the Persians, and in time the Romans would overcome the Greeks. Israel/Judah was a vassal nation. This was, in the words of Zechariah, a "day of small things" (Zechariah 4:10). Tensions are such that soon after your time guerrilla warfare will break out.

The hymns you are choosing as a compiler have been composed over a long period. Some of them may even go back to the time of David himself. But that is not your concern. Like a modern hymnbook compiler, you want to choose hymns that will be sung by the current congregation whatever their origin, that will have meaning for them, and that will coincide with their own ordinary view of what they expect from religion and its liturgy. So, in the sorry circumstances in which you find yourself and your community, which hymns, which psalms, do you choose? Obviously you will want to choose some that speak to the anguish and despair that your congregations must be feeling. You will recognize that some of that grief is particular to your people at that time, and some is simply part of the human condition. But, like the singers in Liverpool, you will also want to sing hymns that describe your identity as people who have continued in faith when others gave up, or mocked or descended into cynicism. Your praise will be defiant. Like the singers in Liverpool your exuberance will be born of a vision of better times and an unshakeable faith in certain fundamental values.

Like a modern compiler you will no doubt be influenced by the prevailing theological currents of the day. The post-exilic period in which you are working is one of great theological creativity. The Exile experience has sparked a great deal of new thinking about God. In particular, the belief that there is only one God, rather than that YHWH was one god amongst many, has had repercussions. If there is just one God, then that god must be the God of all creation. In post-exilic times, there was a blossoming of creation theology which we can see evidenced in parts of the book of Isaiah, and in the so-called Wisdom literature of the Old Testament. Also, if there is just one God, as well as having a plan for creation, this is a God who must surely have a plan for history. We begin to see books appearing that claim to have access to this plan, which divides history into different ages. These two theological strands, whilst presenting a mind-boggling view of the majesty of God, do not come without problems. If God is God of all creation and all history, then why is there evil in the world and why have things been organized so badly as to allow bad things to happen to good people? As a compiler you will be acutely aware that this is a very current issue, because so much of the material at your disposal raises just this issue. You will also be aware of the popular mood that God has deserted Israel, or at least that God is very distant.

The book of Job, part of the Wisdom literature, is one response to these issues, but there are the beginnings of another theological strand, which will develop and be important for some time. This is the strange form of religious writing we call "apocalyptic". This is a form that seems to have dominated theology from around 180 BCE to the third century CE. Attempted definitions of this genre are usually rather long and complex, in order to encompass the many different examples, but there is general agreement that it originated as a response to situations of oppression, persecution or other kinds of suffering, and as an answer to the human question, why? This is a question first articulated by the ordinary theology of the Psalms. The basic issue in all apocalyptic writing is the faithful incomprehension of those whose experience is at odds with what their faith teaches.

If we take the New Testament book of Revelation as an example of the apocalyptic style, here are people who have been told by their Christian tradition that a great victory has been won by Christ on the cross. But for them, suffering persecutions which may have been local or more widespread, and under what seemed like the unconquerable power of the Roman Empire, nothing much has changed. Like the psalmists, they ask why God is not intervening. What is the point of faith, especially a faith that claims to have universal authority, if it makes no difference at all to their circumstances?

Apocalyptic writing reassures them that the God of all history has a definite plan. They are actually on the cusp of a new age, in which justice will prevail, and they will be vindicated. Certain things must happen to enable the birth of this new age. For instance, the power of evil has to be dealt with. The image of a woman giving birth is sometimes used. The present suffering is like "birth pangs", but the joy of a new age will follow as surely as, in the joy of receiving a new child, the pain of the birth is soon forgotten. In the meantime, the faithful must not give up; they must endure and certainly not give way to either idolatry or immorality. The idea of God in apocalyptic writing is indeed that he is distant, but in a way that makes God more important. He is like the Prime Minister, surrounded by a cabinet of messengers or angels who are responsible for executing God's will for humankind. The Minister of Health is Raphael, of Defence/Warfare is Michael, of Communication is Gabriel—you get the idea. Then there's a Minister without Portfolio, known in Hebrew as the wandering Rover, or Satan. Apocalyptic writing attempts to shift the resolution of injustice in the world to the important future time when the new age dawns. It will be accompanied by a judgement, with God as judge, which will redress wrongs.

In this way of thinking, songs play an important part in the process of seeing evil off. In his commentary on Revelation, John Sweet writes, "In ancient religion hymns, especially *new* and secret ones were thought to have power to rescue man from his earthly prison (Jonah 2; Acts 16:25f.) and open the gates of heaven. The praise of God in itself weakens Satan's power. For *new* is not just fresh but connoting the New Age, which in Judaism was linked with Psalm 98:1 as a reference to the messianic era" (Sweet 1979/1990, p. 129; original italics). In other words, songs, for the suffering, are not just an entertainment, or an accompaniment to a verbal liturgy, or a way of covering movement in a service, as they are nowadays in churches. They were seen as powerful and instrumental ways of "shouting evil down".

They were the football anthems of the ancient world. The relationship between worship and apocalyptic writing is complex but fascinating. Revelation has more references to songs of worship than any other New Testament book, so much so that some scholars have thought that its structure is based on some form of liturgy. What we can say is this: apocalyptic writing is an attempt to answer the questions the psalms ask, and so as a compiler you will need to make sure that those questions are clearly stated. You will reflect the contemporary idea of justice. You will also want to make sure that in the midst of all these universal questions about good and evil, the particularity of Israel is not lost. What does it mean, now, to be Israel? It is a question you may want your psalms to explore.

In a strange way, the idea that Satan could somehow be subverted through music continued into modern times. The oft-quoted "Why should the Devil have all the best tunes" is variously attributed to William Booth, founder of the Salvation Army, and an earlier Methodist, George Whitefield. The basic idea here is that some secular songs and dance tunes, thought by some in Victorian society to be symptoms of sinfulness, could be neutralized and used as weapons in Christian "warfare". It is notable that Booth's mission started amongst the most disadvantaged in society and was named as an army, and that the songs it produced should be understood as weapons. If we think of the psalms as deriving from *ordinary* life and imagine that their original longings came not from the glorious settings of cathedral choirs but rather from the downtown missions of Victorian London, or even the OTT settings of the new songs in Liverpool, they do take on a different complexion. And, like those Victorian hymns, defiant songs can inspire and reassure. The point is that religious songs are not nursery rhymes. They have power, which frequently derives from a context of desperation. They are sometimes, perhaps even often, less expressions of confidence, than defiant expressions of faith in the face of the evidence.

This is a book of six attempts to see the Psalms from a different perspective. The convictions that led me to write it are these:

- Although we use psalms more than any other biblical resource in public worship, they are effectively hidden in plain sight. We include psalms in our liturgies with little understanding of why we do so, and with little attempt to imagine ourselves as part of a history of worship. We do not know why they are there, and we have little understanding of how we can connect with them.
- Scholarship on the psalms has not helped us. They have been read in ways that are pastorally useless. They have a social and psychological context which should be unearthed, and which is related to their context-in-use, rather than their origins or literary character. There have been few attempts to explore connections between our religious

experience and that of these early worshippers. We should instead be asking questions about whether our particularity finds echoes with theirs.
- The use that we do make of them can actually pervert the intentions and character of the psalms through editorial omissions and selections, which often detach individual psalms from their context.
- Psalms is an incredible database shining a new light on to the ordinary religion of ordinary worshippers. This offers us a means of connecting with its hymns, earthing them anew in our experience, perhaps helping us in our own struggle to understand God.

It is all too easy to imagine a golden age of religion and to envy those we suppose to have been part of it. The contention of this book is that this golden age is illusory and that, throughout history, faith has often been at odds with lived experience, and people of faith have often felt under siege in various ways. That is the subject of our first chapter, which concludes that in the face of all that should deny the validity or efficacy of religion, the psalms present us with the voice of ordinary religion, which we categorize as defiant.

The second chapter notes that ordinary religion uses words to describe God like refuge, rock and strong fortress, and the chapter explores what it is that God is a refuge from. Fundamentally, it is the fear of chaos and meaninglessness. The relation of this anxiety to the psalms that speak of creation is explored.

The third chapter wonders how we respond to the times when ordinary worshippers experience the absence of God. There are times stated quite clearly in the Psalms when God does not appear to listen, to notice, to hear or even to care. The psalms offer a defiant response to those who mock the faithful with the charge that there is no God.

Fourthly, we look at the subject in which "official" religion and ordinary religion seem farthest apart: namely who is to blame when problems occur. The official view is that misfortune is largely the fault of human beings who are tainted by sin. The view of ordinary religion is the defiant belief that actually it's God's fault and that God has a case to answer.

The fifth chapter is about human society and how it is governed and maintained. In other words, what we would now call politics. For the psalmists, questions about politics are intimately connected to the king, who is meant to be the embodiment of a covenant that guarantees peace, justice and prosperity. How has that worked out then and thereafter? We see the defiant response.

Our final chapter is about the last stand for the defiant—Jerusalem. The conversation considers the importance for ordinary religion of a sense of place and a sense of occasion.

Each of these sections is headed by a title taken from a familiar hymn. This is to emphasize the links between the ancient worshippers and ourselves. We are not so much observers or the disinterested curious, but rather participants. These are things that matter for the ordinary faithful today. The hymns chosen come from different traditions, and some may be more familiar than others. Some readers may find it helpful to preface their reading by looking through the words of the hymns, though that is not essential. If the book is used as a group study, the hymn referred to, either said or sung, may be a good way to start a particular session. At the end of each section there is a "conversation with God", in the form of a reflective prayer drawing on some aspects of the theme of the preceding conversation. Perhaps (and hopefully) these will encourage further thought and prayer. If the book is being used by a group, these prayer conversations may prove to be helpful summaries and may prompt discussion.

The book originated as a series of Lent talks, and it is suitable for use in groups in that way. However, its theme is not specifically Lenten, and it could be used by book groups or study groups at any time, as well as individuals. I have avoided a structure which includes exercises or reference to text not printed, or questions to consider, in the hope that the book may also be useful as a relatively short read for interested individuals and as an encouragement to preachers. To that end I have kept endnotes and references to scholarly works on the

Psalms to a minimum. I hope that those who come to this book with prior knowledge of those sources will recognize the scholarship that lies behind the writing, and that those who do not will not be frustrated by insufficient reference. I do not want to write a book about ordinary theology that is inaccessible to ordinary theologians.

The book is dedicated to my god-daughter Rita Vidiakin, and her remarkable parents, George and Regina.

CHAPTER 1

Gather us in

Were the people of the Old Testament happy? By "the people of the Old Testament" I mean the people it's all meant to be about: the people of Israel, the ordinary people, the people of the land, the people like us. Were they *happy*? That's an unusual question that we are unlikely to ask, but when we do ask it, we quickly become aware that the available data is pretty thin. It's hard to escape the conclusion, in fact, that most of what we know about these people is second-hand. We know them through what other people say about them, and the result is to paint them in an unflattering light.

Throughout the Exodus they seem ungrateful, surly and disloyal. At Mount Sinai, they quickly turn to worshipping a golden calf, for example. In the time of the Judges, when they are settling the land, they are portrayed as completely lawless and uncontrolled. Deuteronomy, in a passive-aggressive kind of way, tells them that they should celebrate and remember their liberation (suggesting that the prompt is necessary), and if they don't toe the line the consequences will be dire. The prophets of the eighth and seventh centuries BCE warn that their behaviour and carelessness toward the demands of the Covenant will lead to disaster; prophecies which are realized in the Exile. After the Exile, Ezra 10 sees them bemoaning the fact that they have taken foreign wives; actions that are described as unfaithful, causing Ezra to fast, and essentially putting the future of Israel at risk.

Winston Churchill is supposed to have said, "I believe history will be kind to me because I shall write it." That trenchant quote reminds us that people who narrate histories are as much storytellers as other writers. The way they present their characters and the events in which they are involved is often designed to fit a wider agenda. The story of the people of Israel is told by prophets, kings and, particularly, narrators with an agenda. The long history from Joshua through to 2 Kings, for example, along with the book of Deuteronomy, is written as an answer to the question: why did the Exile happen? The author(s) of this account of history believe that it was basically the people's fault, aided and abetted by a sequence of seriously underqualified kings. The history that extends from 1 Chronicles through to Nehemiah and Ezra is written to answer a different question: how can Israel survive the trauma of the Exile with its national character intact? In both cases, the people are portrayed as part of the problem rather than as the victims they have surely been.

There are glimpses of a different story from time to time. For example, in 1 Kings 10, we read about the visit of the Queen of Sheba to King Solomon. This is royal propaganda at its most effective. This A-list celebrity has nothing but praise for the king, based mostly on what she sees of his material wealth. She says, "Happy are your wives, happy are your courtiers ... Blessed be the Lord your God who has delighted in you and has set you on the throne of Israel" (1 Kings 10:8,9). However, a couple of chapters later, when Solomon dies, a delegation of "all the assembly of Israel" comes to Solomon's son Rehoboam, the new king, and implores him to lift the "harsh labour" and the "heavy yoke" that Solomon had laid on his people. In fact, Rehoboam refuses to do that and instead makes life even more harsh: "My father made your yoke heavy, but I will add to your yoke; my father disciplined you with whips, but I will discipline you with scorpions" (1 Kings 12:4,14). So is it possible, apart from these few glimpses, to see how the people really express their feelings: to see what matters to them, what they are concerned about and what religion does for those who are not given great wealth and many foreign wives.

Fortunately, there is a source that tells us just that. It is called the book of Psalms. This unique book gives us an insight into the religious lives of the people, which is not to separate their religious life from the rest of their lives. Their religious life, anyone's religious life, is a way of interpreting lived experience in the light of faith and trust in God. Psalms shows us how they tell their own stories, how they understand meaning in their own circumstances, and the part that God plays in their lives. Quite often it is subversive, telling a completely different story from that which the kings, prophets and official commentators want us to hear. In a sense, we might think of it as the social media of the Old Testament and, like social media, the expressions are often rough, ready and robust. We see their reactions to the faith they have been taught and the traditions they have learned, and the way that is applied to their experience day to day. Their reactions and their outworking of their own "ordinary" theology bears a striking resemblance to our own day, and that is a function of Psalms that is often missed.

So, to return to our original question in the light of this source, were the people of the Old Testament happy? Our initial instinct may well be to say, of course. In as much as we think about the psalms at all, we may well see them as happy songs of praise, sung by a devout people whose faith we often envy. That response is partly due to the fact that although the psalms are part of every service in many traditions, and although, publicly, we probably read the book of Psalms more than any other book of the Bible in our liturgies, we remain largely ignorant about them. Few sermons are preached on the Psalms. After a service, the likelihood is that the psalm that was said or sung is the least remembered part. Words of introduction to the psalm in public worship that might give it some context are non-existent in most churches, at a guess. We have no real idea, if we're honest, what we are reading and why. Hence the title of this book. The psalms are hidden in plain sight or, to use another idiom, buried. We see only the gravestone.

Drilling down a little further, there is a more fundamental reason for our ignorance about the Psalms—an ignorance that is (hopefully) not the case with regard to the Gospels, for example. And that is to do with the tools that scholarship has given us to understand and interpret the Psalms. A recent survey of scholarship on the psalms across the centuries has concluded that it has proceeded without reference to the obvious fact that they are used as expressions of faith by religious communities. In the early days, the psalms were collateral damage in a dispute about who "owned" the Old Testament. Was it Judaism or Christianity? This led to a bizarre and centuries-long argument about whether the psalms were written by David or Jesus (in a pre-incarnational role), and so whether their references are to David or Jesus. The superscriptions at the head of some of the psalms, which are late additions, attempt to relate them to incidents in the life of David, as part of this argument. Even when scholars decided that they were written over a probable eight-hundred-year period, and that they were collected after the Exile to be used in the second temple, scholarship was more interested in them as literary works than as real-life liturgy, speculating about the origins of particular symbols, the metre of

Hebrew poetry and the exact translations of poetic words.

Scholars did manage to get excited about one series of psalms that made reference to the king. In the early and mid-twentieth century, there was lively debate about the kind of service these psalms were used in. Debate centred around whether, when the psalmist says, "The Lord is King" (as in psalms 93, 97, 99, for example), the reference is to something that has just happened, or something more generally true. But that has little to do with the life of a liturgical community nowadays. Study of the Psalms became more like anthropology than theology. People do not come to church because they have a vague curiosity about the rituals of ancient societies. They come because they want to find out more about God, more about faith communities, more about themselves and what it means to be human. And this connects us to those people of the Old Testament because the Psalms bear witness to those motivations and activities. For them, as for us, church services are occasions when, through access to God in the quiet of prayer, in word and sacrament, we can explore those things in the company of others and in a "safe" space—a space that respects and values that quest.

In the late twentieth century, things took a turn for the better. At the beginning of the century, there was the first attempt to classify the psalms. Until then, the book had been regarded like some modern hymnbooks, in which hymns are not classified according to the kinds of occasions when they may be used, but according to some other principle, such as alphabetical order. The book of Psalms has no index. Different kinds of psalm are found side by side in the book. It is divided into five sections like many ancient Jewish books, but scholars have reached no consensus about any principles of organization that this may point to. Around a hundred years ago, a German scholar called Herman Gunkel provided a key tool for subsequent scholarship by listing each psalm according to a type which he proposed. As noted above, that led some scholars to concentrate on so-called Enthronement Psalms, which focused on the role of the king, one of Gunkel's types. However, in the later part of the century, it is perhaps his most striking conclusion that has attracted the attention of scholars. And that is that the most numerous category of psalms in the Psalter is what he called "psalms of lament".

Contemporary scholars such as Claus Westermann have helped us to understand these psalms better (Westermann 1981). They have a recognizable structure that I will summarize thus. They begin with a description of what is wrong. They express incomprehension about the injustice of it all. They make a specific plea to God to intervene. They reaffirm faith in what they have learned about God. They negotiate with God as with a male figure and put arguments to God as to why he should act. They often end with a vow that the speaker in the psalm will praise God or work for God in the community if he shows himself. (I am using non-gender-specific pronouns generally for God, although the psalms themselves are gender specific. The only exception I am making is the substantive "Godself", which I find awkward.) Psalmists may, of course, have been women. A short lament psalm that exemplifies the lament pattern is Psalm 6, which I think could well be understood in a woman's voice:

> O Lord, do not rebuke me in your anger
>   or discipline me in your wrath.
> Be gracious to me, O Lord, for I am languishing;
>   O Lord, heal me, for my bones
>   are shaking with terror.
> My soul also is struck with terror,
>   while you, O Lord—how long?
> Turn, O Lord, save my life;
>   deliver me for the sake of your steadfast love.
> For in death there is no remembrance of you;
>   in Sheol who can give you praise?
> I am weary with my moaning;
>   every night I flood my bed with tears;
>   I drench my couch with my weeping.
> My eyes waste away because of grief;
>   they grow weak because of all my foes.
> Depart from me, all you workers of evil,
>   for the Lord has heard the sound of my weeping.
> The Lord has heard my supplication;
>   the Lord accepts my prayer.

All my enemies shall be ashamed and struck with
terror;
they shall turn back and in a
moment be put to shame.

Interestingly, in the NRSVUE, this psalm is headed "Prayer for recovery from grave illness". That, of course, is a speculative modern editorial description, and ignores the "foes" of verse 7, "the workers of evil" in verse 8, and the "enemies" of verse 10; but it is a departure from the usual biblical superscription which is "a psalm for David". What we do see in this psalm is a description of grief, in some detail. There is the plea to God to save the speaker's life, and a sense of feeling rejected by God. There is the argument that the speaker is no use to God if they die, and there is the statement of faith that the prayer will be answered. Psalm 13 has a similar movement:

How long, O LORD? Will you forget me forever?
How long will you hide your face from me?
How long must I bear pain in my soul
and have sorrow in my heart all day long?
How long shall my enemy be exalted over me?
Consider and answer me, O LORD my God!
Give light to my eyes, or I will sleep the sleep of death,
and my enemy will say, "I have prevailed";
my foes will rejoice because I am shaken.

> But I trusted in your steadfast love;
> my heart shall rejoice in your salvation.
> I will sing to the LORD
> because he has dealt bountifully with me.

This psalm too speaks of enemies, but many lament psalms do. "Enemies" can describe people but can also be a generic term to cover illness, physical pain, shortage of food, a sense of being excluded from the community or betrayal. In this psalm, we see the sense of being forgotten, the negotiation which says God's credibility is at stake in the eyes of opponents, and yet the faith that God's steadfast love will prevail, and the vow to sing to the Lord. Not all laments are so personal; Psalm 12 describes a general despair about the state of society which has a faintly contemporary ring. It describes a society in which good faith between people has vanished; where God's care for the poor is disregarded and where "what is of little worth wins general esteem" (12:8, REB).

All these examples are from the earliest part of the book of Psalms, and that is also notable. Most lament psalms appear early in the book and most psalms expressing praise are late. The book itself mirrors the shape of lament. It could be said to take us on a journey. It begins with complaint and expression of grief but finally realizes the vow to praise.

This "rediscovery" of lament has had two consequences. One has been from the perspective of biblical scholarship. In a 1984 book, Old Testament scholar Walter Brueggemann attempted a new classification of the Psalms (Brueggemann 1984). This was not to undo or question Gunkel's work but rather to find a new "overlay" or critical apparatus that would help to interpret the lament psalms within the whole journey of faith. He identified three stages in that journey and the psalms which were appropriate to each. The first group he called Psalms of Orientation. These were psalms in which the worshippers had a sense of all being well with the world. God had ordered it well and life was good. Sticking to the rules that God had set led to a successful and happy life, of which they were the proof. Psalm 33 would be a good example of such a psalm. However, Brueggemann pointed out that these were psalms sung by those who appeared separated from the grim realities of life. They are appropriate for children to sing, but if sung by adults they speak of denial about suffering and betray a self-righteousness at odds with Christianity.

The second stage is where he locates the laments, and he calls these Psalms of Disorientation, in which the cosy childhood world of order, justice, desert and simplicity is shattered on the hard rock of adult reality, in which bad things happen to good people, and bad people don't get the punishment they deserve. At a personal level, loved ones suffer and die inexplicably. The world is experienced as complex and does not respond to simple answers. Only God can sort things out. Psalms such as 6 and 13 from an individual perspective, or 74 from a community perspective, are examples. Psalm 58 is interesting as it clings to old hopes for natural justice. "It will be said, there is after all reward for the righteous; there is after all a God who dispenses judgement on the earth" (58:11, REB).

The third stage he calls Psalms of New Orientation. These are psalms which tell a story through the earlier stages and have arrived at a more mature understanding of God as a result. Perhaps prayers are perceived as having been answered, or the vow of lament is being paid. Certainly there is a new sense of resolution. Psalm 30 would be such an example. Brueggemann's overlay has been found helpful by many and has encouraged similar attempts from slightly different perspectives. To mention just one, J. David Pleins has read Psalms from a Liberation Theology perspective, and adjusted Gunkel's categories accordingly (Pleins 1993).

Another consequence comes from those interested in Pastoral or Practical Theology who are concerned with the whole concept of lament as having a therapeutic usefulness in contemporary pastoral situations. These might include: a useful form of healing for those who have been abused, those with disabilities, and indeed all those who feel excluded from society because they are different in some "unacceptable" way. The conclusion to be drawn from this work is that we all at some time suffer grief. It is part of the natural human cycle and lament may have a part to play in our healing and reconciliation, our "moving on" and resolution. We need to feel free to address God robustly, to have an avenue for complaint; to have liturgies that find a place for lament, and to rehabilitate the psalms of lament. However, Brueggemann is surely correct in seeing that we cannot simply speak about lament in our worship, in isolation from the rest of it. To do so would be as wrong as the present situation, in which all too often lectionaries edit the psalms we use in church to avoid lament. But I believe Brueggemann does not go quite far enough. He describes, accurately, psychological stages which we go through constantly in our lives, but he does not go on to explore what it means for faith that the whole structure of Psalms assumes a default mode of lament. Mature worship grows from a base of despair.

My experience, both personally, and especially as a pastor, is that the baggage we bring to church often tends to despair. There is political despair about the state of society. The despair that my own views seem to be shared by very few and are ridiculed by many. No political party speaks for me completely and no newspaper completely reflects my views on everything. I think Elijah's feeling that "I only I am left" (1 Kings 19:10) is common. There is despair about the perceived absence of God. What use is our theology (a question asked by Dietrich Bonhoeffer in prison awaiting execution), what use are our prayers when God does nothing to make things better? There is despair about the unfairness of things, deep despair that human nature has plumbed new lows—that the problems are of deeply ingrained and institutionalized sinfulness. There is despair that some of those we hold responsible for the ills of society claim to be acting in the interests of Christianity. There is despair about the superficiality of those who have no respect for creation. There is despair that while I am doing my best and trying to live a Christian life, happiness and success elude me. Just this week a lovely church member of a congregation where I was ministering asked to see me after the service and asked, "Why does God hate me?" It transpired that it was her ability to identify with the psalms of lament that still brought her to church. I think there is a tendency for ministers to assume that people come to church *because* of the evidence. My own sense is that many come *despite* the evidence, despite how the church presents things, despite the liturgy and despite their lived experience. These are the people that I believe the psalms, as a whole, are about.

As Brueggemann's analysis shows, life is not always miserable for everyone. Those are unfortunate indeed who do not experience some happiness in their lives. But as Evelyn Underhill has said, "If it were not for those few brief moments of happiness, life would be perfectly bearable." And the psalms are certainly vehicles for joy and celebration in some circumstances. There is all the difference in the world between singing happy songs about how good life is in complete denial of the suffering all around us (Psalm 37:25) and singing songs about a faithful vision of how life ought to be as an act of defiance; what Brueggemann elsewhere calls "a bold nevertheless".

I think that this calls for honesty about what faith is, at least "ordinary faith" as opposed perhaps to its official version. Perhaps we could call it subversive faith. That is the faith discernible in the Psalms. We too, as ordinary people of faith, often, I think, have a subversive side to our own faith. When we read the official views of religion and society, everything is very definite and organized. Sermons sometimes tell us what we ought to believe. We are prepared for baptism or confirmation with a firm set of doctrines we must uphold. We recite creeds that leave no room for dispute or nuance. In some Christian denominations, the idea of tradition is one which imprisons us in the ways people thought in the past, and that can be very definite and indeed cause problems when dealing with modern social issues. Some churches have a list of beliefs to sign up to or affirm before full admission is permitted. I speak as an Anglican, and as an Anglican I have a different view. We believe tradition is more dynamic, something that results from the action of reason on scripture, and that, I think, reflects faithful people who do not see faith as signing up to a set of definite rules and adhering to an agreed set of beliefs, but rather as being in a relationship with God. The opposite of faith is not doubt. The opposite of faith is fear. Faith is for us a trusting thing, and we can therefore sit quite lightly to many pronouncements from on high, as long as we feel at one with God.

In the Psalms, we see ordinary people who are determined in their faith in that sense. When God appears to act in a way that they do not expect, their response is one of incomprehension rather than rejection of God. That's a view of faith well described in a famous modern parable. It arose during a debate between two philosophers of religion, Anthony Flew and Basil Mitchell, about the nature of faith. Flew saw faith as a propositional thing: something you could express in statements. He believed that in order to claim that those statements are true there needs to be *negative verification.* In other words, you need to be able to say what would count as evidence against what you are claiming. So for someone who believes in God, what would have to happen in order for you to be convinced that you are wrong: the death of a child, perhaps, or some other unjust suffering? Basil Mitchell said that that misunderstood the nature of faith and told this story to illustrate his point:

> In time of war in an occupied country, a member of the resistance meets one night a stranger who deeply impresses him. They spend that night together in conversation. The Stranger tells the partisan that he himself is on the side of the resistance—indeed that he is in command of it, and urges the partisan to have faith in him no matter what happens. The partisan is utterly convinced at that meeting of the Stanger's

> sincerity and constancy and undertakes to trust him.
>
> They never meet in conditions of intimacy again. But sometimes the Stranger is seen helping members of the resistance, and the partisan is grateful and says to his friends, "He is on our side."
>
> Sometimes he is seen in the uniform of the police, handing over patriots to the occupying power. On these occasions his friends murmur against him; but the partisan still says, "He is on our side." He still believes that in spite of appearances, the Stranger did not deceive him. Sometimes he asks the Stranger for help and receives it. He is then thankful. Sometimes he asks and does not receive it. Then he says, "the Stranger knows best." Sometimes his friends, in exasperation, say, "Well what would he have to do for you to admit that you were wrong and that he is not on our side?" But the partisan refuses to answer. He will not consent to put the Stranger to the test. And sometimes his friends complain, "Well if that's what you mean by being on our side, the sooner he goes over to the other side the better."

I quote that story in full because if we are to study the faith experience of Old Testament people, we need to know what they understood by "faith", and in fact the evidence in the Psalms shows that the word "trust" is a better description of it. I think many of us have this in common with them. For many of us faith is not dependent on evidence. By faith we don't mean believing that certain things happened. Rather we mean the things that keep us here in church in the Christian community, namely the sense of relationship we have with God, which is indivisible from hope and love. When we are in a deep and loving relationship we do not ask for evidence. When our partner does something out of character, something we do not expect, our first response is to try to understand what's going on. Faith not only persists without evidence; it persists despite the evidence, evidence that by any rational account would drive us to despair and rejection. And why am I saying all this about faith? Because the psalms give us a window into exactly that kind of situation. A situation where people persist in faith despite the evidence. A situation in which they attempt to work out what's going on. A situation in which they strain to maintain hope against the odds, a state which I want to describe as "defiant faith". Elsewhere I have spoken of the psychological state of the defiant faithful as one of "faithful incomprehension". Most people in long-term relationships will know what I mean.

I find it difficult sometimes, when presiding at a Eucharist service, to find the right words to introduce the saying of the creed. "Let us confess our faith together in the words of the Nicene Creed" doesn't sound right to someone who has just said that faith is not propositional. "Let us declare what we believe" might come closer to it, but it sounds rather awkward. Creeds are legitimate, and it is right that our core beliefs should be affirmed in an objective way. Perhaps there should be some other point in the service where we can simply say "we still trust the stranger".

I think "defiance" describes quite a lot of Christian activity. I think of all those occasions when Christians sing (quoting Psalm 1) "We shall not be moved", or "We shall overcome". I think of the fight against apartheid. I think of Lord Longford continuing to visit Moors murderer Myra Hindley. I think of how our Anglican eye clinic in Aden, in the Yemen, has continued to provide specialist eye care for those who could not otherwise afford it, despite other churches' premises being attacked and personnel kidnapped, in a war zone. It's a facility completely staffed by Yemeni Muslims, and most of its clients are Muslim too, but they are proud and happy to work under a Christian cross, in the premises of a Christian church, and to see us as one "people of the book", existing to meet human need with loving care. Defiant actions, like defiant songs, can be inspiring.

Those who watched the Welsh football team at the Qatar World Cup finals in 2022 would probably say that although they were one of the poorest teams in the competition, they had the best song. It was originally a protest song from the 1980s, written by Welsh folk singer Dafydd Iwan, and it has been adopted by the

Welsh fans. It's called "Yma o Hyd", meaning "We're still here". Its verses go through a catalogue of attempts to wipe out the Welsh culture and language throughout the centuries, but each chorus (in translation) repeats defiantly, "Despite everyone and everything, we're still here." In a very different setting, some, perhaps many psalms are like football anthems. They are defiant songs and songs that only make real sense when they are sung with other people in a crowd. They defy the evidence, sometimes they defy logic, they defy prediction, they say, "This is who we are and where we stand, and we're still here."

Conversation with God

Stranger Lord
I have never had much problem with belief.
I am content to say the creeds, to accept
the verdict of the ages and go along with
statements I barely understand,
sometimes hiding behind their ambiguity.

But faith is different.
Faith is personal, urgent, and important.
It comes and goes, but I cannot
escape it or live without it,
and I always come back to it.
I want to capture it and guard it. I want that certainty.

But it has an elusive quality that confounds
description and defies expectation.

I wonder how "official religion" would
judge my ordinary faith.
How would it mark me?
I think most people believe they would not
score highly, and I would be one of them,
but I hope I'm not a heretic.
I ask questions, but I think genuine curiosity
is a good part of being human.
I do not test my faith against my experience.
I interpret my experience through my faith.

I did not think myself into a way of life. I lived my
way into something that must be thought about.

I think a lot of my prayers must have been
laments, even though I didn't know the word.
All intercession at least, starts with things that
are wrong in the lives of real people in the real
world, things that we yearn to see changed:

injustices reversed,
illnesses healed,
corruption unmasked,
brokenness restored,
warfare and the lust for power replaced
with reconciliation and love.

I suppose all generations would agree that "what
is of little worth wins general esteem".

Always, there is a vision of a better way,
a beautiful serious potential.

Faith is surely the basis of any serious relationship,
and always involves the vulnerability
of acting without evidence.
Who will be the first to say, "I love you",
not knowing what the response will be?

Lord, in you have I trusted. Let me
never be confounded.

CHAPTER 2

Blessed assurance

If we were looking for a single text from the book of Psalms to illustrate the central point of the first chapter, we could do little better than opt for Psalm 31:21:

> Blessed be the Lord!
> for he has shown me the wonders of his love
> in a besieged city (CCP).

or:

> Blessed be the LORD, for he has wondrously shown
> his steadfast love to me
> when I was beset as a city under siege (NRSVUE).

We are all too familiar with what a besieged city looks like from our TV screens, and we can only try to understand from them what it must feel like to live in one. For as many years as we can remember, from Sarajevo and Balkan cities to the devastated cities of the

Levant in Lebanon and Syria, to Aden and the Yemen, and more recently to cities in Ukraine and Sudan, we can perhaps picture ourselves in those situations as we listen to the desperate stories of those who have lost everything and who struggle to survive, fearing every minute for their lives and those of their families. To be able somehow to see, in that situation, the wonders of God's love, is nothing short of an incredible act of defiance that refuses to let chaos have the last word.

Most translations and commentators take the reference here to be a description of the ruined city of Jerusalem, besieged by Babylonian forces in 597 and 587 BCE, equivalent to the pictures and testimonies we see in the book of Lamentations. A more figurative translation is offered by the REB:

> Blessed be the Lord, whose unfailing love for me
> was wonderful when I was in sore straits.

This may lack pictorial imagery, but it may also remind us that at some time most if not all of us live in besieged cities, defying the possibility of chaos. We might experience that chaos today as losing the things that give us security and identity, as in bereavement, redundancy, moving district, a diagnosis of terminal illness, or divorce. These are generally cited as being the most stressful things that humans in our society must face. Or it might mean losing any sense of influence or agency: a sense of being swept along by forces over which we have no control and suspect may be malign. It may include the feeling that the chief influences in the world are indeed malign, and that as a result the world is doomed. Or again, it may be the feeling that everything about life is out of control; that it lacks a structure and meaning. Psalm 89:47 asks, "Remember how fleeting is our life. Have you created all mankind to no purpose?" (REB) Psalm 58 responds, "People will say, 'Surely there is a reward for the righteous; surely there is a God who judges on earth'" (Psalm 58:11). There is an anxiety that nothing holds life together and that it's just a succession of random incidents. Life's a bitch and then you die.

The more usual word to describe defiance in the face of such chaos, in the Psalms, is the word *refuge.* This is clearly a very important word for ordinary theology—the religious experience of ordinary people whose voice we hear almost exclusively in the Psalms. It is a little difficult to add up all the references to refuge in the Bible, because words that can be translated into English as refuge do not always have that exact Hebrew equivalent. The basic root is *chasah*, which gives us the noun *mach(a)s(h)e*, and some other derivatives. That word can also mean trust, in the sense of having confidence in someone. Other words in Hebrew often translated "refuge" include *manos* and *uz*. But if we were to look at an English translation such as the ESV, we find around 89 occurrences of the word refuge, virtually all in the Old Testament. (The possible single exception in the New Testament is Hebrews 6:18). That in itself is interesting because the New Testament does not have an equivalent of the Psalms and is hardly interested in that kind of voice in worship as a source for ordinary theology.

Of the 89 occurrences in the ESV, there is a cluster in Joshua 20 and 21 which deals with so-called cities of refuge. That leaves no less than 44 occurrences of the word "refuge" out of 81, more than half, in the book of Psalms. A word which official Christianity hardly values has been a mainstay of ordinary theology and ordinary piety for hundreds of years. Arguably that is still evident in modern hymnody. In the latest iteration of the Ancient & Modern series, for example, no fewer than 33 hymns correspond to a theme of refuge. They include all-time favourites such as "Jesu, lover of my soul", St Patrick's Breastplate, "Eternal father, strong to save", "O God, our help in ages past", Martin Luther's famous "Ein feste Burg" hymn, "A safe stronghold our God is still", "Rock of Ages, cleft for me", and no fewer than 12 hymns that are based directly on psalms which have refuge as a theme. It seems that we can still be subversive in our hymnody.

Refuge summons up two pictures in my mind. One happened to me on a recent holiday in the Peak District, cycling along former railway routes (you can see what an exciting life I lead). One of these took me through a couple of tunnels, and I was struck by just how narrow these were, and what it must have been like to have been working in one of them as steam trains came hurtling past at 70 or 80 mph. The architects of these tunnels had thoughtfully built small recesses into the wall at various points, and I learned that these were known as refuges, where workmen could shelter when a train came along. As a refuge from a clear and obvious danger they were a good image. But the sense of refuge in chaos I think is better conveyed by water. The sense of being carried along by a torrent, completely at the mercy of the stream, in fear of drowning, and then being able to cling to a branch or hold and climb onto a rock speaks to me of the terror of chaos and the relief of refuge. This image of water is used in the Psalms. Psalm 42:7, for example reads:

> Deep calls to deep: at the thunder of your torrents;
> all your waves and your billows
> have gone over me.

We read something similar in Psalm 69:1,2.

> Save me, O God, for the waters
> have come up to my neck.
> I sink in deep mire, where there is no foothold;
> I have come into deep waters, and
> the flood sweeps over me.

The image of *finding solid ground* is also conveyed in the Psalms with words such as safety and sanctuary; the image of *protection* with words such as shield, and the image of *finding a place of rescue that is safe* by such words as rock and, in some instances, tower or fortress. The most cursory of readings of the Psalms will show that this language is ubiquitous and could easily be identified as one of the main themes of popular piety. As I read it, the refuge is not a copping-out but rather a place for regrouping and taking stock, for which a solid base is needed while we shape a new story for ourselves. In modern usage, refuge can have a variety of references. Outside the world of hymns there is genuine resonance in lived experience with the concept of refuge.

Particularly from where I sit in Cyprus, the concept of refuge is indivisible from that of the refugee. The churches there see a real responsibility towards this group. The Reverend Anne Futcher, my colleague in the Anglican Church, who has a social responsibility brief and deals constantly with the struggles of those seeking refuge on the island, finds a theological basis for her work in the concept of welcome practised by Jesus and articulated, for example, in Matthew 11:28. Jesus invites those in need of refuge to find refuge in God through him. The Psalms invite us all to see ourselves as refugees, people seeking refuge, at some time. It's a concept with many applications.

I well remember, as a young ordinand in theological college, being on the edge of my seat as I listened to an account of ministry from a visiting speaker, Reverend Paul Davies. In 1961, he had been chaplain to the small but devout population of the British Overseas

Territory of Tristan da Cunha in the mid-Atlantic, the most isolated inhabited place in the world. Its nearest neighbour is St Helena, 1,500 miles away, itself remote enough to have been the final place of exile of Napoleon Bonaparte. In 1961, while he was there, the volcano, St Mary's Peak, erupted. Eventually all 264 inhabitants were evacuated. Most came to Britain and were housed in the Southampton area. But life was very different there, and the majority opted to go back in 1963, when it was safe to do so. Around 250 people live there now. Paul explained that it was customary for the islanders to attend morning prayer at the church there on a daily basis and, on this day, with lava falling around them and the sea bubbling, the terrified people gathered to pray. By coincidence the psalm set for the day, he said, was Psalm 46.

> God is our refuge and strength,
> a very present help in trouble.
> Therefore we will not fear,
> though the earth should change,
> though the mountains shake in the heart of the sea,
> though its waters roar and foam,
> though the mountains tremble with its tumult.
>
> There is a river whose streams make glad the city of God,
> the holy habitation of the Most High.

God is in the midst of the city; it shall not be moved;
God will help it when the morning dawns.
The nations are in an uproar; the kingdoms totter;
he utters his voice; the earth melts.
The LORD of hosts is with us;
the God of Jacob is our refuge.

Come, behold the works of the LORD;
see what desolations he has brought on the earth.
He makes wars cease to the end of the earth;
he breaks the bow and shatters the spear;
he burns the shields with fire.
"Be still, and know that I am God!
I am exalted among the nations;
I am exalted in the earth."
The LORD of hosts is with us;
the God of Jacob is our refuge.

He reported that the recital of this psalm was taken as a sign of God's presence and concern. There was calm, and the eventual evacuation took place without any loss of life.

Scroll forward a few years and we find Paul back in Wales, with his wife Evelyn. He has been given a house-for-duty post in a beautiful but remote valley in the Berwyn Mountains at a place called Pennant Melangell. There are just a couple of houses in the valley, but there is a precious church, and it is Paul's job to restore the Romanesque screen it contains which recounts the legend of St Melangell. This seventh-century novice from a local nunnery was walking in the valley when a hare ran under her skirts. It was closely followed by the local prince hunting party. He demanded that she hand the animal over, but she declared that she could not do so because of her Christian profession—a very brave act considering the power difference between them both. It ended well. The prince was so impressed that he decreed that the valley should for all time be a sanctuary for wildlife and that no living thing should ever be killed there again. And so it has remained to this day. Another refuge.

When the shrine was completely restored, the couple wondered what to do next. They lived in a huge vicarage next to the church and Evelyn, who had been working in a hospice, had the idea of creating a place where terminally ill people could come safely for a day, as a kind of respite or even a retreat. Doctors were recruited and necessary work done, and the Cancer Care Centre was born—offering refuge for those suffering from terminal illness. Eventually Paul died and Evelyn became ordained; she had a valuable ministry there and later in Aberdaron, responding to the needs of pilgrims. Thousands go to Pennant Melangell every year, and Aberdaron is the final land stop for those making pilgrimages to Ynys Enlli (Bardsey Island), the reputed burial place of 10,000 Welsh saints. Pilgrimages and retreats offered yet another interpretation of refuge. Psalm 46 had told the story of Paul and Evelyn's lives.

Refuge is a hugely underestimated concept within ordinary piety and theology, and the psalms bear witness to it.

So how else do the psalms act as agents of defiance against the various threats of chaos? The first and most obvious evidence is provided from the laments themselves. Though they often describe desperate circumstances, they nevertheless usually include some statement of faith which, like hope and love, is conveyed habitually in the psalms by the word "trust". The author of Psalm 25, for example, describes their plight thus:

> Turn to me and be gracious to me,
> for I am lonely and afflicted.
> Relieve the troubles of my heart,
> and bring me out of my distress.
> Consider my affliction and my trouble,
> and forgive all my sins.
>
> Consider how many are my foes
> and with what violent hatred they
> hate me (Psalm 25:16–19).

But there is confidence that God will listen and help:

> Lead me in your truth and teach me,
> for you are the God of my salvation;
> for you I wait all day long.

Be mindful of your mercy, O LORD, and of your
steadfast love,
for they have been from of old (Psalm 25:5,6).

I think of these statements of trust as *axioms*. These are the things that I am certain about, come what may. I will defy the evidence of the present circumstance by reminding myself of what I truly believe and have based my faith and worldview on. We also see such statements in the book of Lamentations. It's as if they should be prefaced with the phrase "This I know for certain". Psalm 56 actually uses that template.

This I know, that God is for me.
In God, whose word I praise,
in the LORD, whose word I praise,
in God I trust; I am not afraid.
What can a mere mortal do to me? (Psalm 56:9–11).

Sometimes there is an explanation of the former evidence that led to the certainty, with reference to what has been learned of God's action in the past. Psalm 80 is an example:

Restore us, O God of hosts;
let your face shine, that we may be saved.

You brought a vine out of Egypt;
you drove out the nations and planted it.

You cleared the ground for it;
it took deep root and filled the land.
The mountains were covered with its shade,
the mighty cedars with its branches;
it sent out its branches to the Sea
and its shoots to the River (Psalm 80:7–11).

One of the best-known laments, Psalm 22, which was quoted by Jesus on the cross, has an abrupt change of atmosphere after verse 21. Prior to that the theme is a first-hand account of how it feels to be God-forsaken, but from verse 25 onwards there is defiant praise:

From you comes my praise in the great
congregation;
my vows I will pay before those who fear him.
The poor shall eat and be satisfied;
those who seek him shall praise the LORD.
May your hearts live forever!

All the ends of the earth shall remember
and turn to the LORD,
and all the families of the nations
shall worship before him.
For dominion belongs to the LORD,
and he rules over the nations (Psalm 22:25–28).

Psalm 69, another psalm quoted in the passion narrative, intersperses cries of anguish with axioms of praise in startling juxtaposition:

> But I am lowly and in pain;
> let your salvation, O God, protect me.
>
> I will praise the name of God with a song;
> I will magnify him with thanksgiving
> (Psalm 69:29,30).

Each of these psalms deals with particular symptoms of chaos, but it is notable how others drill down to the heart of the issue, and that means claiming that God is creator. This is the ultimate expression of defiant faith. For those who refuse to believe that the world and all that is in it is just a set of random, chaotic events without meaning or purpose, the ultimate statements of defiant faith and trust are to do with creation theology.

Psalm 74 surveys a devastated city and a devastated temple:

> We do not see our emblems;
> there is no longer any prophet,
> and there is no one among us who
> knows how long (Psalm 74:9).

But verses 12–17 are a defiant reminder of the power of God in creation, with its climax:

> Yours is the day, yours also the night;
> you established the luminaries and the sun.
> You have fixed all the bounds of the earth;
> you made summer and winter (Psalm 74:16,17).

This is a popular form of defiance. Other examples among many in the lament psalms can be found in Psalm 102:25: "Long ago you laid the foundation of the earth, and the heavens are the work of your hands"; and in Psalm 143:5: "The wonders of your creation fill my mind" (REB).

I wonder how we view biblical descriptions and references to creation (where to start)? We might be tempted to turn to the early chapters of Genesis, but there are far more references to creation in the Psalms, and there we can give the whole discussion a context. Far too often the conversation has been framed by nineteenth and twentieth-century controversy between science and religion with questions about how and when—questions the Bible accounts neither ask nor answer. All too often the Church has been content to argue the point on the opponents' ground with the opponents' premises. The point is (as I see it) that creation does not just have a geological structure and language. It does not just have a temporal structure and language, nor does it have a scientifically observable structure and language; it also has a *story*. And once we begin to see the earth, "creation", as having a story, then many other things fall into place. Stories have a beginning and an ending; they have a plot. Importantly for personal faith they have an author. To tell the *story* of the world is to speak of purpose, destiny and meaning, and often to do so in the language of poetry and hyperbole. The world has a narrative structure.

To see the world in this way is the beginning of getting our head round the world, society and ourselves, as a counter to chaos. When the world has a story then we can talk about vocation, relationship, morality, community. We can replace chaos with structure and begin to make sense of things. The antidote to chaos is the story of creation, the world's story, authored by God. In the Old Testament generally, and not just in the Psalms, at times of maximum stress, writers turn increasingly to the doctrine of creation. They laud its strength and wonder at its vastness and variety, and at the privileged place of humanity within it. The book of Job is an essay born of creation theology, setting out how a vision of the vastness of God the creator has superseded primitive mechanical views about natural justice. At the beginning is a narrative section in which a whole series of misfortunes and tragedies afflicts Job, who is a good man and who pointedly has not sinned. His wife is disgusted with the way things have turned out and advises him: "Do you still persist in your integrity? Curse God and die." This is the natural and understandable response, but Job's response is defiant. "You speak as any foolish woman would speak. Shall we receive good from God and not receive evil?" (Job

2:9,10). Earlier he had set out his own axiom: “Naked I came from my mother’s womb, and naked shall I return there; the LORD gave, and the LORD has taken away; blessed be the name of the LORD” (Job 1:21).

It is worth saying at this point that whilst the psalms that use creation theology can be used in defiance of a real-world experience that points to chaos, they can also be used in an unthinking way which speaks not of defiance but rather of denial. One of the drivers in modern times for writers about lament has been the disgust they have felt about churches singing happy songs in a world of suffering and misery to which they appear indifferent. Creation theology can be abused to defend an unjust status quo (apartheid was defended in this way, for example), and to resist social development. The hymn “All things bright and beautiful”, originally written as a children’s hymn to teach about the first lines of the Apostles’ Creed, contains the lines (now not normally sung): “The rich man in his castle, the poor man at his gate; God made them high and lowly and ordered their estate.” In the process of defending the status quo, there is also the danger of maintaining a view of natural justice that favours the well off and privileged, who can come to see their good fortune as part of the order of things, consequent on their being good people.

There is evidence of this in the psalms themselves. Psalm 33 is addressed to “the righteous”. (Can you imagine a service starting with the minister welcoming all the righteous people?) The psalm goes on to describe

God's creative activity and reaches the conclusion that all is well:

> Happy is the nation whose God is the LORD,
> the people whom he has chosen as
> his heritage (Psalm 33:12).

Psalm 37 exudes an air of entitled ones looking to God to deliver them. It has an air of easy confidence:

> Trust in the LORD and do good;
> live in the land and enjoy security.
> Take delight in the LORD,
> and he will give you the desires of your heart.
>
> Commit your way to the LORD;
> trust in him, and he will act.
> He will make your vindication shine like the light
> and the justice of your cause like
> the noonday (Psalm 37:3–6).

Later we read:

> I have been young and now am old,
> yet I have not seen the righteous forsaken
> or their children begging bread.
> They are ever giving liberally and lending,
> and their children become a blessing.

Depart from evil, and do good;
so you shall abide forever.
For the LORD loves justice;
he will not forsake his faithful
ones (Psalm 37:25–28).

This reminds me, in modern times, of people who claim that people are poor through their own fault, and who tend to disregard those less fortunate than themselves. The suffering of the world is reduced to farcical simplicity:

I have seen a wicked man inspiring terror,
flourishing as a spreading tree in its native soil.

But one day I passed by and he was gone,
for all that I searched for him
he was not to be found (Psalm 37:35,36).

It is Brueggemann's conclusion that not only can these psalms be interpreted as cries of defiant faith but that the *only* legitimate use for such psalms is as a cry of defiance, and he is suspicious of churches that "sing songs of orientation in a world increasingly experienced as disoriented . . . It is my judgement that this action of the church is less an evangelical defiance guided by faith, and much more a frightened numb denial and deception that does not want to acknowledge or experience the disorientation of life" (Brueggemann 1984, p. 51).

On the plus side, creation theology has given us the tools of defiance in the Psalms. It has provided us with the narrative of order and structure, and it has assured us of God's interest in us, in a context in which all are equally treasured by God and made in God's image.

It seems to me that the psalms suffer, in our public use of them, from the fact that often we see them as stand-alone pieces, while their arrangement in the book of Psalms may also provide evidence that there is rarely such a thing as an "innocent" song of praise. Take, for example, Psalm 8, on the face of it a stand-alone expression of awe and wonder at the vastness of the universe, and yet also at the fact that humankind has its own integrity within it. But what happens if we look at it from the perspective that it follows Psalm 7? Psalm 7 is a classic lament. It begins by claiming God as refuge, it describes the negative forces in the psalmist's life, it describes the injustice of it all and calls on God to act. The concluding verses speak of the confident expectation that God will indeed act and the final verse is a vow: "I will give to the LORD the thanks due to his righteousness, and I will sing praise to the name of the LORD, the Most High." We then launch into Psalm 8, which is essentially an expanded version of that vow. In other words, Psalm 8 could be read as the inevitable second part of Psalm 7. Some psalms are so connected in different versions of the Psalter, such as 9–10 (in

REB) or 42–43 (in several versions), but this is on literary and linguistic grounds. It is possible, surely, that combinations can be made on theological and formal grounds. In her reception history of the Psalms, Susan Gillingham notes, "By placing particular psalms next to those which have a different style and theology, as well as a different date, each psalm is read not only in its own light, but in the light of its neighbour" (Gillingham, 2012, p. 7).

Once we begin to see the psalms in this way some fascinating possibilities arise. Take 143–145, for example. Psalm 143 is a classic lament which stops short of the final expression of praise. What it has instead is a final expression of servanthood—"I am your servant"—language that is unusual, except in relation to one who holds special office. Psalm 144 is a royal psalm full of expressions of traditional faith which could be seen as an expansion of 143 in that area. It all leads to 145, which is a triumphant song of praise. There are psalms which tell a complete story, from what Brueggemann would call orientation through disorientation to new orientation. That three-stage story can be seen unfolding in, say, Psalm 30 or Psalm 118. But perhaps we can see it unfold, or the lament theme develop and expand, through a series of psalms. This is a largely untrodden path in scholarship, where there have been many attempts to find shapes and patterns in the book's arrangement. At the very least, it is interesting to see how we might see the psalms in a new light by paying attention to their arrangement and sequence in the Psalter.

Even the accepted communal songs of thanksgiving can be seen in a longer perspective. Psalms 64 and 69 are laments. If we see them as bookends, Psalms 65, 66 and 67 are defiant statements of faith, with copious references to creation. They are favourite choices for harvest festivals on that basis. Psalm 66 has an intriguing paragraph of autobiography (vv.16–19) which hints at past trouble and prayer answered. Psalm 68 is an extended prayer for God to act again.

So let us summarize the main points of our journey through the book of Psalms so far.

- The psalms are valuable sources of information about the ordinary faith and ordinary piety of ordinary people.
- That source suggests an underlying experience which is often at odds with what traditional faith has taught. It describes people's anxieties and fears.
- In that context, the language of faith speaks constantly in terms of refuge and trust.
- That from which refuge is sought can take many forms of common experience, but fundamentally one fear is the fear of chaos and meaninglessness.
- One of the functions of creation theology, and the psalms that include it, is to give reassurance that

feeds defiant statements about structure, order and purpose.

- Other axioms of received faith open the way for robust dialogue with God.
- The pattern of lament, once one begins to see it, is a possible key to understanding the shape of the Psalter.

There is surely much to connect that ordinary faith and piety with our own. We too persevere in faith despite the evidence. The concepts of refuge and trust have great resonance in ordinary theology today, and ironically our greater sophistication has made us no less aware of the proximity of chaos and meaninglessness than was the case for these ancient people. We too want to say defiantly that creation demonstrates a vision, whilst at the same time we are aware of all that is wrong in the world as we arrange it. We desperately want to feel at one with creation and at peace in the world, but we want that for all and not just "the righteous". We want to believe and do believe that our lives are more than "life's a bitch and then you die". By being part of God's story, we too feel we have a legitimate context for praise: not denial, not entitlement, not complacency.

We too have our axioms. Sometimes we might feel they are embarrassingly simple. "God is good all the time; all the time, God is good." "In the end all will be well, and all manner of things shall be well." "God is, he is as he is in Jesus so there is hope. God is, he is for me, so it is worth it" (my own favourite, after a former bishop of Durham). I have always been struck by one axiom I first saw on a tapestry banner at the entrance to the then Evangelical Home for Boys in Ramallah, West Bank, Israel/Palestine. The home was then an orphanage (now it's a hotel advertised on Booking.com), but this was 1989, the time of the first Intifada. Danger and violence were everywhere, yet here was a place caring for the most vulnerable victims defiantly standing for a better vision of humanity. The legend read: "It is better to light a single candle than to curse the darkness."

Blessed be the Lord!
for he has shown me the wonders of his love
in a besieged city.

Conversation with God

Refuge God,
perhaps I could survive a besieged city
if I believed it would be rebuilt;
if I had trust in some international
ordered community
like the United Nations
who could set
and maintain the standards of normality.

And when I think of the times I have felt
under siege
drowning
swept along,
what makes it survivable,
What maintains the hope to keep going?
Is it the trust I have
that in some way I can't explain
you have a handle on it all?

I have visited a war zone
just after the fighting stopped.
The buildings were at crazy angles.
The streets were indistinguishable
  from the waste land.
People were carrying bits of wood,
anything that would burn, to keep them warm.
And I heard people singing hymns, defiant.
And it gave me hope.
Not just for them, but for me.

The other day I told my grandchildren
  how I met their grandma.
It was chance.
We both fancied a bacon sandwich in the
  same pub after a night of revision
in our university days.
And I tell them, smiling,

if it hadn't been for the bacon
sandwiches in the Boar's Head
you would not exist.

Is that how life is?
A series of accidents and coincidences?
I do not want to feel like a programmed machine
whose life patterns are inevitable,
but I do need to have a theme to my narrative
that speaks of a loving creator
who wants the best for me
and presents me with options;
and if I take the road less travelled
and get lost,
will find me.

CHAPTER 3

Immortal, invisible

Churches are communities of prayer. It is a great reassurance to church members that they are not alone in the anxiety, suffering or grief that prompted the prayer in the first place. My experience of visiting people in hospital, which I assume is common to clergy, is that the most emotional moment of the visit is often when I say to the patient that the congregation prayed for them at the previous service. Healing services in churches are popular for similar reasons. I remember, when I worked in religious TV for a while, doing an interview with the then Archbishop of Armagh, Robin Eames, on an International Day of Prayer for Ireland. I asked him how it felt that people all over the world were praying for him personally on that day. It was an emotional moment for him, and it took him some time to reply. During the Covid pandemic, shared prayer on digital platforms was almost a survival mechanism for some.

But this sharing of prayer can have unforeseen consequences of great pastoral importance, when one person's prayer is apparently answered and another's is not. Perhaps the circumstances, the objects of the prayers, are similar; for example, during the pandemic, prayers for elderly parents. The initiators of the prayers are devout and sincere. Those who join the prayers make no distinction between them. But one parent recovers and the other dies. In one household, there is rejoicing and God's name is praised. There may even be talk of a miracle. But in the other household things are different. There may be a resolution along the lines that God had different plans and that he wanted this person with him in heaven, and who are we to question God? The Lord gave and the Lord has taken away. But equally there may be unresolved incomprehension, with questions along the lines initially of "why us?" Later, perhaps there will be more reaching questions around whether God really listened, really heard or indeed really cared. This can even create a crisis of faith in God. Is God real? If so, why is God so apparently capricious? Of course, within individual psalms we do not see comparison or competition between outcomes. But an overall view of the Psalms reveals all too easily something we can identify with from our own experience: prayer answered and prayer apparently ignored.

On the one hand, we have the psalms that invite us to rejoice with those who rejoice. Sometimes we see simple statements that tell us that the petitioner prayed, and that the prayer was heard:

> In my distress I called upon the LORD;
>   to my God I cried for help.
> From his temple he heard my voice,
>   and my cry to him reached his ears (Psalm 18:6).

Sometimes it was not only heard but acted upon:

> He asked you for life; you gave it to him—
>   length of days forever and ever (Psalm 21:4).

> For he has delivered me from every trouble,
>   and my eye has looked in triumph
>   on my enemies (Psalm 54:7).

Sometimes there is a little more narrative and context:

> I will exult and rejoice in your steadfast love,
>   because you have seen my affliction;
> you have taken notice of my adversities
>   and have not delivered me into
>   the hand of the enemy;
> you have set my feet in a broad place (Psalm 31:7,8).

> Come and hear, all you who fear God,
>   and I will tell what he has done for me.
> I cried aloud to him,
>   and he was extolled with my tongue.
> If I had cherished iniquity in my heart,
>   the Lord would not have listened.

> But truly God has listened;
> he has heard the words of my
> prayer (Psalm 66:16–19).

Psalm 30 tells a longer story. Initially the writer had felt secure in a simple faith. Then disaster struck, as a result of which the author prayed a simple prayer for mercy. Then something happened to turn the situation around. We are not told what it was, but it had the effect of turning lament into dancing. A similar turnaround is described in Psalm 116:8–10. Here we see also the determined axiom "I kept my faith" and the defiant response the supplicant made to opponents:

> For you have delivered my soul from death,
> my eyes from tears,
> my feet from stumbling.
> I walk before the LORD
> in the land of the living.
>
> I kept my faith, even when I said,
> "I am greatly afflicted".

Of course, intervention, like non-intervention, is an interpretation of events that is prompted by faith. Accounts like those in Psalm 30 and Psalm 116 leave us wanting to know "what really happened". Perhaps it was straightforward: a recovery from disease, for example. Perhaps it was more complex and involved a complete turnaround of fortunes. As the psalms recount these stories, we are reminded that they are human stories from lived experience and that is why we want to understand them. Were these Old Testament *miracles*? We tend to associate miracles with the ministry of Jesus, and to make a big distinction between the Old and New Testaments in that regard. But surely God's action in miracle is not confined to that three-year period?

Nowadays I think we often regard miracles as being like conjuring tricks. Perhaps it was always so. John complains about it in his Gospel. But miracles are basically events that defy logic and expectation and break into despair. Those who hope for miracles, and describe their experience in terms of them, exhibit defiance. They are prepared to be countercultural. I believe in miracles, but I don't think of them as magic. Often, they are acts of unexpected love. There is a poem by Sydney Carter about Mother Teresa caring for a terminally ill man who has simply been dumped on her doorstep. It begins: "No miracle will come in time to save this man's life except the one surprise of being loved". That is how I understand miracle. The story of the Good Samaritan in Luke 10 is a miracle story. It defies convention and shows a boundary-crossing love and care that is totally unexpected, and perhaps not even wise.

A poem by the modern Welsh poet Gillian Clarke illustrates well the way in which the word "miracle" can be used to demonstrate a perceived act of God—an act unexpected and unimaginable. It describes a true story from the 1970s, in which the poet is taking part in a therapy session in a Mental Health unit. The people there are quite ill, and she describes their behaviour in vivid detail that begins with the stark phrase, "I am reading poetry to the insane". Her eye catches one particular man who is big and mild and who is "tenderly led to his chair". This man, it seems, has never spoken. He is a "big dumb labouring man". The action is set at the beginning of March and outside the room the daffodils are in full bloom. In the midst of her reading, this man suddenly stands up, and no one is quite sure what is going to happen. What does happen is that the man who has never spoken recites Wordsworth's poem, "Daffodils", word perfectly. Everyone claps. The poet tries to work out what has happened. Perhaps the man had learned the poem long ago in a valley school in South Wales, and the recital of poetry has prompted something in his memory. But the effect was to lift the whole occasion and to give it new significance. Clarke calls the poem "Miracle on St David's Day".

Perhaps this was the kind of thing that made the difference in the story of Psalm 30. I believe in miracles. I believe in angels (this is not just a list of chart hits from yesteryear, but even they bear witness to something in the human imagination). Perhaps it was human intervention interpreted as an act of God that changed things unexpectedly. Or perhaps it was a simple reassuring word, or perhaps a prayer resolved in some other way. All these possibilities connect *us* to the story of Psalm 30. It could be the story of any of us. "I love the LORD because he has heard my voice and my supplications" (116:1) could be the response of any of us.

Sometimes the story a psalm tells is not about an individual but rather a story about a whole community or even "the nation". Psalm 107 has a liturgical feel. It is divided into four sections. Each section describes a group of people in trouble. On each occasion, the psalm says, "Then they cried to the LORD in their trouble, and he delivered them from their distress." Then in each of the four cases the psalm invites a congregational response. "Let them thank the LORD for his steadfast love, for his wonderful works to humankind." It is tempting to locate such communal songs of thanksgiving within the history of Israel as far as we know it. There's a suggestion that Psalm 107 could refer to returning exiles. "Some wandered in desert wastes, finding no way to an inhabited town; hungry and thirsty, their soul fainted within them" (Psalm 107:4,5). "Some sat in darkness and in gloom, prisoners in misery and in irons" (Psalm 107:10). Some were fools who took to rebellious ways, and some were caught in sea storms (unlikely for returning exiles). In each case there was a good outcome and an invitation to thanks and praise.

One scholar writes of these psalms of thanksgiving generally: "The Psalms of Thanksgiving empower us to continue the search for a worship that will deepen our experience of the God of history, the God of those who are in misery and sorrow—a God who speaks to injustice, poverty and suffering on a community and global scale. If our liturgies have offered real comfort to the beleaguered, shown gentleness to the distressed, opened a space of joy in the midst of suffering, then we shall have moved beyond worship as a spectator sport toward a worship that has each worshiper actively engaging the life-and-death struggles that give depth and hue to our entire planet" (Pleins 1993, p. 73).

More simply, in these psalms we can imagine the details of the human stories that gave rise to them and relate our own experiences to theirs. These stories tell our story. This gives worship, and praise in particular, a seriousness which it sometimes lacks. These are serious, defiant songs. Thinking of the Clarke poem, if we simply described the last act of the poem, the depth and significance of that act would have been missing. "Man recites 'Daffodils'" can simply mean someone appreciates what a lovely view there is from his room.

However, we are not only encouraged to rejoice with those who rejoice in the Psalms, but also, and more frequently, *to weep with those who weep.* Alongside these stories of God's interventions and prayers answered, there are other glimpses into the experiences and feelings of those who have no sense of the presence of God; no sense that their prayers are even heard. Psalm 13 begins:

> How long, O LORD? Will you forget me forever?
> How long will you hide your face from me?
> How long must I bear pain in my soul
> and have sorrow in my heart all day long?
> How long shall my enemy be exalted
> over me? (Psalm 13:1,2).

The tone of those whose experience is of an unheeding God is, as we might expect, more urgent and anxious. However, we might be shocked by the robust addresses made to God. God is constantly asked quite roughly "How long" it will be before God gets his act together, (Psalms 13:1,2; 35:17,22; 62:3; 74:9,10; 79:5; 89:46; 90:13; for example). God is told to:

> wake up! Rouse yourself for my defence,
> for my cause, my God and my
> Lord! (Psalm 35:23).

The "roughness" of this request is often hidden by a translation that uses the English word "arise". This sounds terribly polite and is much better than the "get off your backside" approach which is the general tenor of the request. On other occasions God is accused of not wanting to get involved, or of having a tin ear:

> Why, O LORD, do you stand far off?
> Why do you hide yourself in times
> of trouble? (Psalm 10:1).

> Rouse yourself! Why do you sleep, O Lord?
> Awake, do not cast us off forever!
> Why do you hide your face?
> Why do you forget our affliction and
> oppression? (Psalm 44:23,24).

> Do not be deaf to my weeping (Psalm 39:12 REB).

One familiar and immediate way in which people can be assured of God's interest is through prophetic oracles, but sometimes the community looks in vain for that kind of intervention. God is not even speaking through his prophets:

> We do not see our emblems;
> there is no longer any prophet,
> and there is no one among us
> who knows how long.
> Why do you hold back your hand;
> why do you keep your hands in your
> pockets? (Psalm 74:9,11).

Perhaps the most telling criticisms of God (for these are really what they are) are those that challenge God's nature:

> You keep my eyelids from closing;
> I am so troubled that I cannot speak.

> I consider the days of old
>   and remember the years of long ago.
> I commune with my heart in the night;
>   I meditate and search my spirit:
> "Will the Lord spurn forever
>   and never again be favourable?
> Has his steadfast love ceased forever?
> Are his promises at an end for all time?
> Has God forgotten to be gracious?
> Has he in anger shut up his
>   compassion?" (Psalm 77:4–9)

Needless to say, the "official" view, that we are encouraged to take and remember, does not see it like this. God has no case to answer: quite the reverse. Jeremiah 8 could well be described as God's lament. It is the mirror image of the psalmists' lament:

> Why then has this people turned away
>   in perpetual faithlessness?
> They have held fast to deceit;
>   they have refused to return.
> I have given heed and listened,
>   but they do not speak honestly;
>   no one repents of wickedness,
>   saying, "What have I done!"
> All of them turn to their own course
>   like a horse plunging headlong into battle.

> Even the stork in the heavens
> knows its times,
> and the turtledove, swallow, and crane
> observe the time of their coming,but
> my people do not know the ordinance
> of the LORD (Jeremiah 8:5–7).

And that passage continues in the same vein. Just as with the lament of the people, God also has axioms, foundational statements about God's nature:

> I am the LORD; I act with steadfast love, justice, and righteousness in the earth, for in these things I delight, says the LORD (Jeremiah 9:24).

However, our chief interest is in the psalms, and their expressions of ordinary piety, and for them the perceived absence of a caring, involved God is crucial. As the above examples show, this perceived absence can lead to a crisis of personal faith, but defiance fights against this as the petitioners try to persuade God that what is really at stake is God's own credibility in the eyes of sceptics or, as they are described from the very outset, "scoffers" (Psalm 1:1). It is easy, as we read through the Psalms, to ignore the references to these scoffers, and to other groups of antagonists described as adversaries or enemies, but once we become aware of them, they are sufficiently ubiquitous to suggest that they are major players in the lives of the faithful. I wonder how we picture these people. Perhaps we think of them in a military context: that they are people physically engaged in some kind of warfare; but usually the military image is just that—an image. These enemies are described as such by what they say or how they act or respond to another's ill fortune. If we take Book 1 of the Psalms (Psalms 1–41) as an example, we are introduced to these enemies or foes of God in a number of ways; many will be recognizable from contemporary experience.

There are those who deny what is, for the faithful, as we have seen, a core belief that God is a sure refuge. Psalm 3 is typical:

> O LORD, how many are my foes! Many are rising
> against me;
> many are saying to me, "There is no
> help for you in God" (Psalm 3:1,2).

Clearly, it is what they say that defines them:

> For there is no truth in their mouths;
> their hearts are destruction;
> their throats are open graves;
> they flatter with their tongues (Psalm 5:9).

Psalm 35 gives a much fuller picture. The images draw on a wide variety of settings. Verses 1–3 use the image of armed conflict, one of many images and not to be taken as a defining context. Verse 4 imagines an assassination plot. Verses 7 and 8 describe ways in which hunters might trap their prey, with nets and pits. Verse 11 has the language of a court trial, with malicious witnesses. Verses 12–14 revert to the language of ordinary life as the petitioner recalls how, when the enemies were in trouble, he prayed for them and cared about them. Verses 15 and 16 describe a crowd jeering when he "slipped".

There is something euphemistic about the language of slipping in the Psalms, and it is intriguing to know what it might stand for. Psalm 38:16 describes another slipping that enemies rejoice over, for example, while 94:18 tells us that God's love holds him up when he is in danger of slipping (see also Psalm 18:36). Psalm 73:2 says that the psalmist had almost slipped when he saw how the wicked prosper but 73:18 then describes how the enemies will be placed on slippery ground as a judgement.

Psalm 35 continues to build images. Verse 17 describes opponents like lions who would tear him apart. This is an incredible picture of someone who feels under siege. In verse 23, we have the call to God to wake up and vindicate him (in some undisclosed way) so that these enemies will no longer shout hurrah at his downfall (verse 25) but will themselves be judged. This is the typical response to this sense of being part of a beleaguered community of faith. On the one hand, there is the call for God to do something for the petitioner—usually to provide some evidence that God has heard and understands their plight. On the other, there is the call for God to judge the opponents, and the axiomatic assurance that in the end they will be judged and justice will be done. Faith will have been seen to be worth it.

The theme of judgement is the major theme of Psalm 37. A clue as to the setting is provided in verse 7. "Do not envy those who gain their ends, or be vexed at their success" (REB). A defiant claim is made: "But the LORD will laugh at the wicked, for he sees that their day is coming" (v.13). In the meantime, the problems of the psalmist are the problems of God's credibility. The opponents have successful lives and can afford to scoff at those who do not and yet trust in God. Psalm 41 is pathetic in the way it describes the isolation of the sufferer and the cruelty toward him on the part of those who have no time for God:

> My enemies wonder in malice
> when I will die and my name perish.
> And when they come to see me, they utter empty words
> while their hearts gather mischief;
> when they go out, they tell it abroad.
> All who hate me whisper together about me;
> they imagine the worst for me.
> They think that a deadly thing has fastened on me,
> that I will not rise again from where I lie.

> Even my close friend in whom I trusted,
> who ate of my bread, has lifted the
> heel against me (Psalm 41:5–9).

Similar sentiments are expressed in Psalm 31:11–13.

It is notable that both the first and last psalms in this Book 1 collection refer to enemies. Psalm 40 also describes those who "seek to take my life" and "desire my hurt." Here too there are those who cry hurrah at the psalmist's downfall. But defiantly, his faith prompts him to conclude:

> But may all who seek you
> rejoice and be glad in you;
> may those who love your salvation
> say continually, "Great is the LORD!"
> As for me, I am poor and needy,
> but the Lord takes thought for me.
> You are my help and my deliverer;
> do not delay, O my God (Psalm 40:16,17).

So, can we picture the kinds of situation from which these prayers, these psalms derive? The evidence we have so far consists of the faithful incomprehension of those who cannot see why God does not intervene in what is obviously a just cause. Suffering is portrayed in a variety of images, sometimes violent, that seem to point to social isolation, illness, poverty and incapacity. Nevertheless, there is the defiant belief that God will hear and act, despite the derision of those who do not have faith in God yet appear to have more successful lives. There is the belief that in the end those people will be judged and those who suffer now will be vindicated. There is also a suggestion (see, for example, Psalm 25:3) that for some this has just been too much, and they have given up on faith. Psalm 18:25 could be seen as a defiant axiom in those circumstances: "With the loyal you show yourself loyal."

In addition, there are more aggressive responses. The "name-calling" is reversed as the opponents are accused of being idol-worshippers in Psalm 115:4–8. Although these people are introduced as "nations" (see also 31:6 and 135:15), the sentiments echo, on behalf of Israel, what we think individuals might feel towards those who trust in other gods. After all, it is one of the chief complaints that the God of official religion, as seen in the prophets, especially Ezekiel, has against the people of Israel—that they follow foreign gods.

But perhaps the most interesting aggressive response is towards those who say there is no God. This is the heart of the defiance. This is the fundamental defence against a view that there is no justice, no order and no structure; that there is no narrative, and so no author. As we have seen, the "evidence" of creation is appealed to, and the "fact" of Israel as a civilized nation can also be cited as part of the defiance. There remains the name-calling of those who might entertain the irrelevance of God. They are fools.

We normally associate the title "fool" with the book of Proverbs, where the fool is the one who makes the wrong choices as opposed to the wise. However, there are passing references to fools in the Psalms. Sometimes English versions translate the Hebrew word *kesil* as "fool" (as for example 49:10; 92:6; 94:8). The more precise meaning there is "self-confident", as opposed to one who places their trust in God. But the most defiant full-frontal attack on fools, as those who would undermine the most basic axiom of faith, is to be found in Psalms 14 and 53, which are virtually identical. Perhaps this was an oversight by compilers, gathering psalms from different sources, in which case it would suggest that this is a particularly popular psalm, with its dramatic opening line: "The fool has said in his heart there is no God!" It is worth further examination.

The Hebrew word used here is *nabal*, whose root meaning is emptiness. A fool is an empty person. As we read that opening line today, we are probably reminded of modern atheism. We might think of atheists who come from a scientific background and believe truth has to be evidence-based (rather like the philosopher referred to in Chapter 1), or from a Humanist background, who cannot believe in transcendent reality. We are perhaps reminded of those excruciating public debates between Christians and atheists, in which the latter portray Christianity with the same degree of nuance and insight that someone who has never played cricket might use to describe it to those who have never seen it played. That is not what is being described here.

In fact, the Old Testament devotes a whole chapter to help us to understand what amounts to a worldview summed up in this epithet, fool. I like to think of it as a Mr Men story.

For those unfamiliar with the Mr Men stories by Roger Hargreaves, they are a preacher's dream. They personalize concepts like happiness or meanness into the characters of Mr Happy or Mr Mean, and then tell a story in which they act as that character—a modern creative take on incarnation. There is also an equivalent female series of Little Miss stories. The Old Testament has a story about being a fool, being a *nabal*. In 1 Samuel 25 we have the story of Mr Nabal. This story hinges on his name, and like the original Mr Men books it illustrates the concept well and does so in a most entertaining way:

> Mr Nabal is rich. He has 3,000 sheep and 1,000 goats, apart from property. From the get-go, he is described as surly and mean. The story of which he is a part concerns David when he is on the run from Saul. Very politely, David sends messengers to Nabal to ask him for some help. His men are hungry. They need a neighbour, and it seems David's men have already been helpful to Nabal's shepherds. They see Nabal, who is consumed with the business of shearing, and

they make their incredibly (almost comically so) polite address. Nabal simply sneers at them and sends them away. He accuses David of being no better than a runaway slave who should be sent back to his master. His property is his and no one else is having any of it.

Nabal's wife Abigail sees all this. She is the perfect opposite of Nabal, described as beautiful and intelligent. She realizes that when David gets this rebuff, he will be angry and it will not end well, so she secretly packs up mule loads of supplies and goes to meet David to try and head off disaster. She finds him setting out to massacre the entire household, angry at the response he has received. But David is charmed and mollified by Abigail. She refers to her husband as "this wretched fellow. It's no good talking to him. Nabal by name, nabal by nature," (1 Samuel 25:25). David declares a blessing on her good sense. Their whole conversation carefully involves references to God's plan. Their shared worldview involves God at every turn, in comparison to Nabal. She goes home to find that her husband is drunk as the result of an end-of-shearing party (!). When he sobers up, she tells him about the narrow escape they have had, and he is so shocked he has a heart attack and dies. Then Abigail marries David. A lovely story, but I have a feeling I know this man.

> I know where he lives. I can anticipate what he's going to say or tweet. I know what paper he reads. He is the man who can dismiss God, because he thinks he has the power to do so. He has wealth, probably people defer to him, he has power. He has influence. He is self-contained. What more could God do for him? He probably thinks he deserves his good fortune and has worked hard to get it, and that those who are poor deserve what they get too. Nabal is also *kesil.* On the one hand the fool is full of himself. On the other, he is a picture of emptiness. It's not so much that God doesn't exist. For him, God doesn't matter.

But Psalm 14, with its dramatic beginning, is voiced by people for whom God does matter; the people for whom God is their only comfort and the ground of their hope. These are people who have no power, who are at the mercy of others' decisions, and whose only defiant faith is that God sees, and God sympathizes, and God "remembers". The psalm is in two parts. The first part seems to condemn the whole human race, but the second part makes it clear that it is those "who devour my people as if eating bread, and never call to the Lord" (Psalm 14:4) who are the objects of judgement. And that is what this psalm is about: us and them, where the "them" is the Nabals of this world who appear to hold all the cards and have no need of God. Its theme is not a philosophical debate about the existence of God. Its theme is justice and the gulf between those who are self-sufficient enough not to need God, and those for whom God is their only refuge.

Scoffers, enemies and adversaries people the Psalms, and their very presence poses a threat to people of faith. The scoffers are not remote intellectuals. They are people who experience life satisfactorily without God. The evidence for their approach can be overwhelming and leads both to the urgent, earnest pleas that God should act, and also to the defiant put-downs that we see in the Psalms. Their attitude is associated with wickedness and greed as seen in Psalm 10:3,4:

> For the wicked boast of the desires of their heart;
> those greedy for gain curse and
> renounce the LORD.
> In the pride of their countenance the wicked say,
> "God will not seek it out";
> all their thoughts are, "There is no God."

Either they will be proved wrong, and God will act, and the evidence will be there—as it is for some who can rejoice over their answered prayer—or judgement will come to them in the end. In the meantime, their life is without substance. What kind of life is it that can ignore the vastness, grandeur and design of creation? What kind of life is it that can ignore the things that make for relationship, community and society? What kind of life does not have love at its heart? The lives of the fools are, as their name suggests, empty. This is a defiant claim.

We can applaud and support them but of course we are not like them. But we are not like Nabal either. Perhaps in the story we are more like Abigail—people who can read situations and realize their consequences, but who additionally have the humility to pray and to recognize God's presence in the humble poor, to know something more about God because of that, and to celebrate that presence in the assembly of the faithful.

And so, for the compiler, this is an important voice for you. It arises from the general feelings of near despair that afflict society generally but has specific reference to individual misfortune of the faithful and the verbal abuse that people who have abandoned faith in this "useless god" throw at them. Your collection generally emphasizes the laments of both individuals and communities but also provides resources for defiant hopefulness. Little would you know that over 2,000 years later your work, if not generally ignored, would be used to give a superficial happy gloss to people living in complete denial of the tears of the world.

Conversation with God

Listening, remembering God,
at least as my hope pictures you,
am I a fool?

Am I a fool to think you hear,
to think you care?
Or am I a fool who is self-sufficient enough
for it not to matter?

I believe in miracles.
I find them difficult to discern sometimes.
I once baptized a little girl
they said was terminally ill.
It was in her home,
with her family and cousins
on her seventh birthday, and we had a party
that brought laughter and value
to that dreary council house, on a
dreary estate in a dreary town.

I see her now, skipping around the room
with a funny hat
hiding her bald head
and everyone saying, "You'd never know."

And the thing was,
the cancer left her.
I was embarrassed to be honest,
to think, as people thought
that there was a connection.
"It's a miracle," they said.

I enquired about the girl
after I left that parish.
She had two years of unexpected life.
But she died in the end.
But I think, looking back,
there was a miracle there somewhere.
It's just that I'm not sure where.
Am I a suggestible, gullible fool to think such things?

I suspect rather that I am at my most foolish
when I think I am at my strongest.
Insights generally come to me, truths
  are evident to me most clearly
in my times of weakness and brokenness.
Angels come at times like that, I think.
If I must boast, says Paul,
I will boast of the things that tell of my weakness.
And he was no fool.

Lord I believe:
Help thou my unbelief.

CHAPTER 4

Just as I am

I'm sure we were all sad to hear of the death, in 2023, of Chaim Topol, the Israeli singer. He made his name as Tevye in the film and play *Fiddler on the Roof*, and is remembered particularly for one song—"If I were a Rich Man". The song reasons and negotiates with God. If he were a rich man, there would be all sorts of things he could do that would benefit God as well as himself: he could "sit in the synagogue and pray", or "discuss the holy books with the learned men, several hours every day". His poverty was a bit of a mistake, according to the song. It could easily be remedied, without it spoiling "some vast eternal plan". This kind of easy chatter with God has a long history in Judaism, and in so far as it contains a covert negotiation, it forms an integral part of lament. Indeed, the whole tenor of Tevye's conversation is reminiscent of the Psalms.

In the conversations between God and humankind in the Old Testament, it is usually God's speech, either directly or through an intermediary, that predominates.

We know what God thinks about everything. We know God's intentions, frustrations, regrets, commitments and vision. Most of the other side of the conversation is assumed. In the Psalms we hear the other side of that conversation, and we find, unsurprisingly, that in addressing God, ordinary people use ordinary language and idiom. We have already seen that this can be robust and direct, even colloquial, and that prompts interesting questions about the power dynamics involved and about how ordinary people viewed God. The psalms consist largely of the human side of conversations with God. They differ from many modern hymns in that respect. Only a minority of hymns take that form of direct address nowadays. It is far more common to have hymns that are expressed in the third person or that are addressed to the Church or to Christians.

As we have noted, the common wisdom is that the psalms were created over a period stretching back perhaps as far as the time of King David (around 1000 BCE), including pre-exilic, exilic and post-exilic contributions. "Gradually psalms were organized into groups and then into collections, each given a heading to connect one with another, and later still these collections would have been incorporated into the five different books which make up the Psalter as a whole" (Gillingham 2012, p. 7). The Psalter finally reached the form in which we know it by the third century BCE. Some early psalms are believed to have been repurposed from Canaanite originals (such as 29 and 68). Others are dated in terms of their references to the king, the temple and Jerusalem. This means that the God who is addressed in the Psalms is understood differently throughout a period of some seven hundred years and hugely differing circumstances, and that is not at all clear from casual reading. It might be said, however, that while different theologies were developing in the Old Testament as we know it, the ordinary basic understanding of who God was and what God represented in the minds of popular piety did not appear to change that much. God, however understood by the theological parties and interests of the time, was still the refuge; still the defiant stand against chaos and meaninglessness; still the one to whom valid prayer could be made.

Perhaps the main development we see in the Psalms is one from a polytheistic understanding to a monotheistic one: from a world of many gods in which the God of Israel was the best, to an understanding that saw Yahweh as the only God and hence the God of all creation, the God of all history and the God of all peoples. Psalm 82 is an example of the former understanding. The scene is set thus:

> God has taken his place in the divine council;
> in the midst of the gods he holds
> judgment (Psalm 82:1).

The psalm compares God (here given the older name Elohim in Hebrew) with other gods. They have different distinguishing features. God judges the other gods in a way that displays God's own nature:

> How long will you judge unjustly
> and show partiality to the wicked?
> Give justice to the weak and the orphan;
> maintain the right of the lowly and the destitute.
> Rescue the weak and the needy;
> deliver them from the hand of the
> wicked (Psalm 82:2–4).

Obviously other gods have no interest in the weak and needy. It is interesting that the name by which God reveals himself does not describe a specific function. Ancient gods often have names that suggest their field of interest. The name by which God wants to be known is YHWH, usually pronounced Yahweh. This is a name which opens up the possibility of a universal and all-embracing God:

> God said to Moses, "I AM WHO I AM." He said further, "Thus you shall say to the Israelites, 'I AM has sent me to you.'" God also said to Moses, "Thus you shall say to the Israelites, 'The LORD, the God of your ancestors, the God of Abraham, the God of Isaac, and the God of Jacob, has sent me to you': This is my name forever, and this my title for all generations" (Exodus 3:14,15).

This is a different kind of name. Its full translation in Hebrew could be "I am who I am, and I shall be who I shall be". Some theologians (notably Walther Zimmerli) have seen this as a key text:

> The God who is invoked by the name "Yahweh" repeatedly demonstrates his freedom by dashing to pieces all the "images" in which humanity would confine him. This takes place not only in Exodus 3:14, in the account of how the divine name is revealed to Moses, but to an equal degree in the great prophets, or in the realm of wisdom, in Ecclesiastes and Job (Zimmerli 1978, p. 14).

That being said, there is no concept in Hebrew of a God who simply "is". There is no way in Hebrew to debate the existence of God in the way that medieval theologians did. Hebrew language is built around verbs. It is only possible to think of a God who "does", a God who acts. Hence God's inaction, as we saw in the last chapter, provokes a real crisis. But however God is addressed in the Psalms, the ordinary faithful's expectations of God do not change. They expect God to be as the Covenant describes God, whose nature is the source of truth, love, justice and mercy. God's *presence* is described in different ways. At some times, God's action is discerned in creation, at some times in his creation of Israel. At some times, God is to be found in some sense in his king, at some times in a special holy place such as Jerusalem, or even within the worshipping congregation. With such changes it is remarkable that God can continue to be addressed as Tevye addresses God in the familiar way that one might speak to a friend, albeit one whose seniority deserves some acknowledgement. God is the one with "the vast eternal plan".

So, let's look at the vast eternal plan as the Old Testament wants us to read it. Effectively it's a story about disobedience and its effects; the effects of human shortcoming and sin. It's a narrative that puts ordinary human beings in a very poor light. Disobedient Adam, the grumbling ungrateful people of the Exodus, the lawless Judges period with unspeakable abuses, the accusations of the prophets of the eighth and seventh centuries about the sinfulness of society, and the descent to Exile.

The fact that we accept this as "the truth" is a triumph for one of the main Old Testament editorial sources. Scholars know it as D (for Deuteronomy). The way of thinking represented by this source began before the Exile and is to be found in the book of Deuteronomy, the books from Joshua through to 2 Kings, and in the teaching of prophets like Jeremiah. After the Exile, in a "we told you so" sort of way, the D writers set out to write a history to determine why the Exile happened, which would conclude that it was our fault, the people's fault—aided and abetted by some poor kings. The Exile was a punishment for sin. It echoed the story of the flood. God had lost patience, had had enough. It was time to bring an end to Israel as it had existed and start again, as Isaiah puts it, after:

> she has served her term . . .
> her penalty is paid . . .
> she has received from the LORD's hand
> double for all her sins (Isaiah 40:2).

Human disobedience led to everything going wrong. Strangely, some scholars accept this without question, even though the Old Testament does have other traditions. Ah, they say, the people of Israel sinned. They got what was coming to them.

However, if you were the equivalent of poor Mr and Mrs Jones at 33 Mount of Olives View, Jerusalem, it didn't seem like that at all. And the psalms shine a light here onto a major difference, not only between the accepted narrative and ordinary experience, but also between the view of the Old Testament faithful and their New Testament counterparts—and their Christian successors, including us. Because the dominant view of the Psalms is not, "We have sinned and deserve all we get (but fortunately God is gracious and loving and forgives and redeems us)"; rather it is, "We don't deserve this. We deserve better. It's not our fault. God is not keeping his side of the bargain he struck with us; he's forgotten us and let things slip. He's asleep again." Who's at fault and what's to be done about it are matters for the psalmists' conversations.

Psalm 26 is quite blatant. It begins, "I have led a blameless life: test me and try me" (REB), and continues:

> I do not sit with the worthless,
> nor do I consort with hypocrites;
> I hate the company of evildoers
> and will not sit with the wicked.
>
> I wash my hands in innocence
> and go around your altar, O LORD,
> singing aloud a song of thanksgiving
> and telling all your wondrous deeds
> (Psalm 26:4–7, NRSVUE).

The psalmist is a regular in church, a shining example of faithfulness, but there is a veiled warning that all this is called into doubt by God's lack of recognition:

> Do not sweep me away with sinners
> nor my life with the bloodthirsty,
> those in whose hands are evil devices
> and whose right hands are full
> of bribes (Psalm 26:9,10).

The end repeats the main statement: "I lead a blameless life."

Psalm 17 is a lament that calls for justice. The psalmist's prayers are innocent of deceit:

> If you try my heart, if you visit me by night,
> if you test me, you will find no wickedness in me;
> my mouth does not transgress.
> As for what others do, by the word of your lips
> I have avoided the ways of the violent.
> My steps have held fast to your paths;
> my feet have not slipped (Psalm 17:3–5).

It is with this confidence, this negotiation, that the psalmist has the confidence to urge "Rise up, O Lord" in verse 13.

Psalm 66 describes a resolution like this: "I lifted up my voice in prayer, his praise was on my tongue. If I had cherished evil thoughts the Lord would not have listened, but in truth God did listen" (Psalm 66:17,18).

Psalm 44:4–8 is a description of faithfulness; in this case the faithfulness of the community. But verses 9–16 are a shocking indictment of God. God has humiliated and deserted them. But (and here we see the negotiation) "All this has come upon us, yet we have not forgotten you or been false to your covenant" (Psalm 44:17). On this basis, the psalmist can have the confidence to say:

> Rouse yourself! Why do you sleep, O Lord?
> Awake, do not cast us off forever!

> Why do you hide your face?
> Why do you forget our affliction and oppression?
> For we sink down to the dust;
>   our bodies cling to the ground.
> Rise up, come to our help.
> Redeem us for the sake of your steadfast
>   love (Psalm 44:23–26).

In the eyes of all these worshippers, the ordinary people, God has a case to answer. This is completely unfamiliar to modern Christians, who can only interpret these remarks as hubris, because as Christians we are used to taking the rap. In many traditions, each service of worship begins with a confession, and usually these go out of their way to lower the petitioner's esteem. The 1662 Common Prayer confession for Morning and Evening Prayer enjoins us to confess "our manifold sins and wickedness". And the confession that follows is hardly complimentary:

> We have erred and strayed from thy ways like lost sheep, We have followed too much the devices and desires of our own hearts, We have offended against thy holy laws, We have left undone those things which we ought to have done, And we have done those things which we ought not to have done, And there is no health in us.

Historically, Christians have been urged to express their wretchedness even more fervently. Consider this prayer from Calvin's "Forms of Prayer for the Church":

> And surely, O Lord, from the very chastisements which thou hast inflicted upon us, we know that for the justest causes thy wrath is kindled against us; for, seeing thou art a just Judge, thou afflictest not thy people when not offending. Therefore, beaten with thy stripes, we acknowledge that we have provoked thy anger against us: and even now we see thy hand stretched forth for our punishment. The swords which thou are wont to use in inflicting vengeance are now drawn, and those with which thou threatenest sinners and wicked men we see ready to smite.
>
> But though thou mightest take much severer punishment upon us than before, and thus inflict blows an hundredfold more numerous, and though disasters only less dreadful than those with which thou didst formerly chastise the sins of thy people of Israel, should overtake us, we confess that we are worthy of them, and have merited them by our crimes (quoted by Sölle, 1975, p. 9).

This masochistic ritual could not be farther from the sentiments of Psalm 26. But has ordinary religion changed that much? Really, do we seriously own up to *crimes* every week? Do we really believe that we deserve to be beaten to pulp on a regular basis because of the evil things we do? I very much doubt it. This kind of confession has become almost completely ceremonial. Ordinary religion wants to have a place to confess human shortcoming and the things of which perhaps we are ashamed or regret; but that is surely evidence in itself that we are not morally bankrupt. We have, hopefully, moved on from a view of life which sees us as morally superior to others, but the chances are that deep inside, what we really want to say echoes Psalm 26: "I'm not that bad and I'm doing my best." Ordinary faith does not see religion as being completely about sin.

The plain fact is that, on behalf of ordinary religion, the psalms feel able to reflect a dialogue between humankind and God which understands that the relationship is such that it is legitimate to challenge God's apparent administration of justice. Psalm 73:13 betrays a common feeling that religion needs to be "worth it". "Indeed it was all for nothing I kept my heart pure and washed my hands free from guilt" (REB).

These examples fall within the "negotiation" phase of lament, which includes other arguments about how things ought to be different, apart from appealing against the injustice of it all and challenging the attempt to paint humanity as continually in the wrong. Psalm 139:16 appeals to the record:

> Your eyes foresaw my deeds, and they
> were all recorded in your book;
> My life was fashioned before it had
> come into being (REB).

The idea of a record of our good and bad deeds being kept is here combined with a hint at predestination. The former is closer to Islam than Christianity, though it did have a medieval life in the idea of the Treasury of Merit. This was the scheme that saw each of us as having a kind of heavenly bank account that was continually in debit. However, the account balance could be made up by the excess merits of Christ and the saints. This idea persists in those prayers that end, "through the merits of Jesus Christ our Saviour". Psalm 139:16 also contains the assumed question, "If I am unacceptable in some way, why did you create me like this?" Verses 13–16 of the psalm describe how wonderfully and carefully God has fashioned each of us, making this a legitimate question, and one that is asked in contemporary society by those who have until recently found themselves at odds with it on account of their sexuality or gender.

A further dimension is added at Psalm 89:47, which asks, in effect, why did you set us up to fail? In other words, is there really a vocation for each of us, and is there really purpose in creation? "Remember how fleeting is our life! Have you created all mankind to no purpose?" Also, part of these conversations is the negotiation that corresponds to bargaining. Commonly it runs along the lines: I could be so useful to you if you let me live. What use to you am I dead? (Psalms 6:5; 35:17,18; 71:20–22; 88:10 are a few examples among many.)

This is all completely alien to the mainstream message of the *New* Testament:

- The God who freed slaves from oppression in Egypt has become the God who frees all humans from the slavery of sin.
- The God who saves good people from trouble has become the God who saves bad people from sin.
- The God who stands accused has in effect become the accuser and judge. The Christian petitioner is now the accused.

This is largely to do with the new view of God presented to us in Jesus and the new estimate of God's power this necessitates. No longer do Christians think God has the power to change everything and order the world as it should be. Rather God's power is evidenced as the power to forgive and the power to redeem. (This assumes people who need forgiveness and redemption.) Lament is now "officially" redundant (according to New Testament writers). The answer is no longer to respond to unjust suffering by complaining to God, it seems. Now Christians are encouraged (as at 1 Peter 2:20–24 for example) to endure their suffering as a kind of witness, and so to copy the action of Christ, finding consolation in the knowledge that he understands our sufferings.

There is one collection of psalms that more closely corresponds to a recognizably Christian view of penitence. They are sometime called "Pauline" psalms because their view of sin appears close to that described by Paul, especially in Romans. This view of sin was given greater prominence by St Augustine and was eagerly seized upon by the Reformers, who were only too ready to adopt a penitential mode in response to what they saw as the corruption of the then Western Catholic Church. There are just seven of these psalms in the Psalter, and they have been identified as Penitential Psalms since the writings of someone called Cassiodorus in the sixth century. They are Psalms 6, 32, 38, 51, 102, 130 and 143. Probably the best known are Psalms 51 and 130. Psalm 130 is often used at funerals (and is a set psalm in some funeral liturgies), and Psalm 51 is used extensively in penitential liturgies and appears more frequently in the Revised Common Lectionary, where its most familiar use is as the set psalm for Ash Wednesday. In the 1662 Book of Common Prayer, in the Morning and Evening Prayer invitations to confession, three of the verses cited are from Psalm 51 and one from Psalm 143. Psalm 51 begins:

> Have mercy on me, O God,
> according to your steadfast love;
> according to your abundant mercy,
> blot out my transgressions.
> Wash me thoroughly from my iniquity,
> and cleanse me from my sin.
> For I know my transgressions,
> and my sin is ever before me.
> Against you, you alone, have I sinned
> and done what is evil in your sight,
> so that you are justified in your sentence
> and blameless when you pass judgment.

This is confession as Christians nowadays would recognize it. In this psalm alone do we have such a familiar response to sin. The superscription to this psalm is interesting. The superscriptions have not featured much in our discussion to date; scholars see them as added at a late date, often linking them to David and to events in his life. This psalm is linked to the story of David and Bathsheba in 2 Samuel 11,12, and particularly to the part where Nathan the prophet convinces David of his sin. The king says, "I have sinned against the Lord" (2 Samuel 12:13). Nathan then tells him that he will not die and that another will die in his place. Although there is probably no historical link between the psalm and the story, it is clear that this is meant as a real-life example, a case study of how the penitence described in Psalm 51 operates. So "David, an *abased, failed self*, now becomes *a restored self*, even in the context of his lost son" (Brueggemann 2014, p. 110, original italics). Confession leads to forgiveness and restoration.

Martin Luther believed that the theological point of these Penitential Psalms is that God's grace overwhelms the reality of sin, perhaps most evidently in Psalm 102. Psalm 143 is a confession of a kind: "No living person is innocent before you" (v.2). But here there is a greater description of what a forgiving God looks like. All the verbs—listen, answer, let me know of your love, show me, deliver me, teach me, guide me, revive me, release me—are expressions of humility, expressions of an acceptance of a relationship between God and humankind that we would recognize as Christian. And yet there is no sense that this attitude and the one we have been describing are at odds with each other. There is no name-calling. Penitents do not call out the folly of those who see injustice in their plight. The author of Psalm 143 accepts their wrong. Others can see no wrong; they see only injustice. Does this not describe us at various times? Certainly as a pastor, I have lost count of the number of times I have heard that cry of injustice. What did he do to deserve this? There is of course a time for confession, but perhaps there is also a time for defiance. Perhaps it's not an either/or.

Of the remaining Penitential Psalms, Psalm 32 is the one that most overtly speaks of the release that confession can bring:

> While I kept silent, my body wasted away
> through my groaning all day long.
> For day and night your hand was heavy upon me;
> my strength was dried up as
> by the heat of summer.
> Then I acknowledged my sin to you,
> and I did not hide my iniquity;
> I said, "I will confess my transgressions to the LORD,"
> and you forgave the guilt of my
> sin (Psalm 32:3–5).

As I have noted, it has often struck me that the expression in Psalm 6 could sit better in the mouth of a female than a male and that perhaps we need to challenge the accepted wisdom that all these psalms were written by men. We know that women did compose and sing; the song of Deborah in Judges 5 is thought to be one of the oldest traditions in the Old Testament. The Exodus song in Exodus 15 is gender neutral and there is specific reference to the song of Miriam (joined by other women) in verse 21. Hannah's song in 1 Samuel 2:1–10 is sufficiently well known for Luke to reference it as he records the Magnificat. Women also sing and dance in 1 Samuel 18:7. Some scholars believe the Song of Solomon was written by a woman. I have a hunch that other psalms may reveal new meanings if we imagine them on the lips of women. There has been a suggestion that Psalm 55 was written by a rape victim.

This chapter has maintained and developed the theme that the psalms are songs of defiance. They are songs that are derived from personal fears and anxieties about chaos and meaninglessness; they are songs in defiance of scoffers and adversaries, but they are also songs of defiance directed towards God. They are songs that boldly accuse God of failing to meet God's own standards of justice and mercy. They are songs that defy a default view that humankind is morally bankrupt, and instead they say, "We're better than that and you should notice." They are songs that are defiantly unafraid to hold God to account.

This view is clearly at odds what has come to be accepted as the Christian view of the relationship between God and humankind. The interesting question is, which is closer to the view of contemporary ordinary religion? With which view do we most associate nowadays ourselves? My own pastoral experience leads me to think that a belief in natural justice such as Old Testament people held, and which gives them the right to question God, is persistent. In the New Testament, we see a concerted attempt to dissociate disease, sin and punishment. John 9 is perhaps the place where this is most overt. But in the popular mind the connection is still often made. I have lost count of the number of bereavement visits I have made to hear grieving next of kin tell me that the deceased did not deserve to die in the way s/he did. In the 1980s, there was a bizarre example of whole communities taking the view that HIV was a punishment from God for what members of those communities perceived as the sin of homosexuality. This was a view that tabloid newspapers loved to highlight. They used terms like "gay plague" to connect HIV with biblical plagues and managed to find individuals from the religious community to put the view forcibly. Famously in 1985 *The Sun* ran a headline, "'I'd shoot my son if he had AIDS' says Vicar", complete with a picture of a vicar with a shotgun.

I think it is also true that, as Psalm 77 says, people think religion should be worth it. In other words, the reward element is as important as the punishment. Apocalyptic writers were particularly interested in this and developed the idea of a final judgement after death. This judgement would right the injustices of life as we know it. An unintended consequence of that view is to make the "worth it" element of religion more or less a future issue in a way that could not be corroborated. The destiny of the dead came to assume, through much of Christian history, an importance that outweighed the quality of life in the present. Life after death became a credal element of Christianity to an extent that the Jesus of the Synoptic Gospels would have difficulty in recognizing it as the heart of his good news. Sin came to assume an importance in terms of judgement, evidence that large parts of the New Testament were at pains to play down. The view of 1 Peter that unjust suffering should be borne patiently is one that is largely drowned out.

Humankind likes to have tidy systems, and the psalms we have been looking at in this chapter bear that out. It is worth remembering that the book of Job was written specifically to counter any view that constricts God to human organization. "I am what I am, and I shall be what I shall be" means just that. God is not part of a predictable system. This clearly provides frustrations for ordinary religion, which nonetheless proceeds as if it were otherwise. Sooner or later, though, these ordinary beliefs collide with experience, and not just the confected ones of Job. Most of the psalms of lament reach some resolution. Negotiation has taken place, God will hear, God will act; his name will be praised and all will be well. That is the nature of defiant faith. But two psalms, 39 and 88, have no such resolution.

Both are reminiscent of the book of Lamentations in which, in faithful incomprehension, the people describe the horror of what they perceive God has allowed. Throughout the whole book we are just longing for God to respond, but no response comes. Psalm 39 describes someone who does not give up. Even though he says to God, "I am exhausted by your hostility" (Psalm 39:10 REB), he continues to pray to the end. Psalm 88 paints a grim picture. The psalmist has suffered from childhood (88:15). He prays morning, noon and night (88:1,2,9,13) but hears nothing. His negotiation is one of the most bitter:

> Do you work wonders for the dead?
> Do the shades rise up to praise you?
> Is your steadfast love declared in the grave
> or your faithfulness in Abaddon?
> Are your wonders known in the darkness
> or your saving help in the land of
> forgetfulness? (Psalm 88:10–12)

The answer to each of these rhetorical questions is no, and all that is left is to accuse God, in the final poignant verse:

> You have taken friend and neighbour far from me; darkness is now my only companion (88:18, REB).

And we might ask why this person has persisted so long. Lamentations 3:24 gives a hint of an answer to someone else who feels their prayer has been rejected. "The Lord, I say, is all that I have; therefore I shall wait for him patiently" (REB).

The fundamental problem of the relationship between God and humankind is introduced in the first 11 chapters of Genesis, and it is there that we are invited to contemplate the importance of sin. The question is, will human sinfulness fatally undermine God's good creation or, rather, will God's grace overcome human sinfulness? That is the ongoing question throughout the whole of our Bible, and Psalms articulates it without solving it. On the one hand, we have expressions of human potential as part of and, in a sense, the pinnacle of creation:

> For it was you who formed my inward parts;
>   you knit me together in my mother's womb.
> I praise you, for I am fearfully
>   and wonderfully made.
> Wonderful are your works;
>   that I know very well.
> My frame was not hidden from you,
>   when I was being made in secret,
>   intricately woven in the depths of the earth.
> Your eyes beheld my unformed substance.
> In your book were written
>   all the days that were formed for me,
>   when none of them as yet existed
>   (Psalm 139:13–16).

And on the other, we have the Penitential Psalms.

Changing views of God have some positive results. God is both praised and blamed. As God of all creation, God can be praised and relied upon to guarantee order. But as organizer-in-chief God can also then be blamed for all that goes wrong. The record of the Psalms, predominantly, is of those who persisted in faith despite the evidence. That gives the ordinary faithful confidence to bargain and negotiate with God. But that negotiation is, of itself, of no effect to one who will be what God will be. Defiant faith does not give up, but the vast eternal plan will not be gainsaid.

The problem of justice remains. Remember, this is a people who are being told that the Exile is evidence of God's judgement on them as a people. But if God is a just god, the psalms demand that God judge their opponents too. They are happy to offer themselves now to the judgement of God, as we have seen, but part of their despair is about moral chaos, and defiant belief in a moral, just God is an important response, then as now. I remember attending a seminar as a TA Army Chaplain once in which a senior Infantry Officer was describing his faith. He said it could be summed up in a sentence: "I believe that the man upstairs will see to it that the evil bastards get their come-uppance" (sic).

The apocalyptic theology that developed around the second century BCE to the third century CE makes a contribution here. It may seem that in this world bad behaviour and sin go unnoticed and unpunished, but there will be a Day of the Lord, and that will be a day of judgement when all will get what they deserve. From that base, the idea of a Last Judgement gained traction. No one would escape that, not even the dead, who for most of the Old Testament were thought to have simply retreated into oblivion in Sheol. There would be a resurrection, heralding a new age and marking a time of judgement. Most of this judgement theology appeared after the publication of the book of Psalms; but we see in the Psalms the urgent questioning, and the demand for such an outcome. There are over a hundred references to God's judgement in the Psalms. That judgement will not only "clear" the names of the devout, but will also condemn those who believe there is no accountability. Such a belief provides a defiant defence against moral chaos. It has passed into Christianity in its essence. The question about accountability is one we still recognize and, I think, one with which we still struggle.

Conversation with God

Forgiving and redeeming God,
Paul mused about the human condition,
and found moral choice a problem.
I muse about the human condition
in the light of your revelation as it has been to me
and find moral choice a gift
that no other part of creation enjoys;
a privilege.
There are some who see the role of religion as
to discipline, constrain and regulate
humankind.
And there are others,
and I count myself among them,
who see its role differently:
To enable, to encourage and to inspire.
In other words,
I believe in the power of grace,

and consider it stronger than sin.
Augustine made things worse
I think.
What is "original sin" except a negative
    way of describing us
that we can do nothing about?
And when we, mechanically, impute it to the newborn,
it seems like a curse from a wicked fairy,
rather than a gift from a loving God
who decreed we should be as we are.
How can I believe in a God who would punish
    us for what God created us to be?
And how can God be angry?
How can God be wrathful?
When anger is itself a sin?
That is how I muse.
Like Leonard Cohen I believe the light
    gets in through the cracks.
But is such musing
simply a symptom of my own sin?
I wonder.
And I am glad that I have the gift of wondering,
and deciding,
even when I am wrong.
I praise you for I am fearfully and wonderfully made.

CHAPTER 5

Sing we a song of high revolt

In March 2023, for a weekend, the world of sports reporting on the BBC was thrown into turmoil. *Match of the Day* presenter Gary Lineker had been suspended, and colleagues had refused to work in protest. What Gary had done was to ignite the age-old debate about how political decisions and rhetoric could be publicly criticized on moral grounds. The football commentator spoke out publicly (on Twitter) about the Government's immigration policy, and said the language being used to commend the policy was reminiscent of the rhetoric of Nazi Germany in the 1930s. For a whole weekend, the arguments raged between the Government and the BBC about free speech, and the underlying message to Gary Lineker was that he should "stick to sport. Don't get involved in politics." On the following Monday, the Thought for the Day speaker on Radio 4 was the Bishop of Manchester, David Walker, who speaks for the Church in the House of Lords on matters of social policy. He said he had something in common with Gary

Lineker. He too had been told many times to "stick to religion" and not to stray into the field of politics. He went on to point out that that is something impossible for active Christians to do, since both Christianity and politics have a common interest in the wellbeing of the populace, the ordering of society, and the administration of justice. Christianity has an interest in the viability of society and maintains that for a society to be successful it must have integrity and morality at the heart of its governance. For those of a certain age, this may well have struck chords with situations in the 80s and 90s. Then, the Church was viewed almost as the official opposition to the Government, with a high public profile on a variety of matters such as nuclear disarmament, apartheid in South Africa, the North–South Global Divide, and how to respond to the Falklands conflict. The then Archbishop of Canterbury famously accused the Government of creating and presiding over "a pharisee society".

Clearly Lineker's comments struck a chord. His suspension was the first item on most weekend news bulletins. This was evidence of what earlier I described as "political despair", the sense that decisions are being made in my name that I not only do not approve of, but indeed abhor, and am censored for venting my disapproval. This provides evidence for me of a society in decline. Political despair is allied to an anxiety about the direction in which society is moving, and about whether society as such can even survive. During the same period, ordinary people were moved to glue themselves to motorways in protest at the Government's policies on climate change. Conspiracy theories abounded about a supposed suppression of any comments that could imply that the Government's handling of the Brexit process had been bungled, and an environmental group named itself in expectation of human extinction. I suspect, though, that there has usually, if not always, been a sense of despair about the way society and the world are ordered. I remember a parishioner telling me how she had suffered acute post-natal depression in the early 1950s when the Korean War was raging, and the Hiroshima experience was still alive in the public mind. She had felt despair at bringing a child into such a world, which surely, she felt, could not last long.

Nowadays that sense of despair extends, in the view of many, to the Church itself, in its response to the situation. Then, back in the 80s and 90s, it seemed to many of us that this engagement with society was a way in which the Church understood itself and its mission. A whole generation of Christians grew up with that self-understanding. Now there appear to be other priorities and other definitions of mission are dominant. Then there was an atmosphere of hopefulness that a better vision would prevail. Now (and with the advent of social media) there is a sense of a "last stand" for the despairing.

There is a biblical equivalent for this understanding of a faith community. The basic concept is summed up in the term *remnant*. For many, now, ours is a remnant church. There is a pathetic picture of a remnant understanding of a faith community in 1 Maccabees 4:45,46. Judas Maccabeus and his brothers had won a military victory that enabled them to enter Jerusalem. There they found the temple area overgrown and in ruins. They decided to demolish what was left of the consecrated altar, "defiled by the Gentiles". The account continues:

> So they tore down the altar and stored the stones in a convenient place on the temple hill until a prophet should come to tell what to do with them.

The remnant is there to preserve things. It is there to preserve traditions, stories, places that embody faithfulness, places where "prayer has been valid" for a time when once again they can be brought to life and be a full part of the identity of the community, and once again point to God's presence rather than God's absence. It was a remnant community that decided to gather together the traditions that we now call the Law and the Prophets; and it was a remnant community that gathered together, and presumably used, the Psalms that are the object of our study. Surely this is something we have in common. Psalms, in their use at least in post-exilic times, belong to a remnant ecclesiology, a remnant view of the faith community, such as the one we now inhabit.

However, the idea itself is ultimately hopeful. No matter how bad things get, God preserves a remnant. Gathering the traditions has revealed that it is part of God's character to do so. The story of the flood provides a remnant in Noah and his family (Genesis 7:23). When there is a terrible famine in Egypt during the time of Joseph, God has a plan to preserve a remnant (Genesis 45:7). When Elijah fears that the religion of YHWH is finished, God reassures him that a remnant will remain (1 Kings 19:18). When it looks as though Jerusalem will fall during the siege of Sennacherib, Isaiah quotes 2 Kings 19:4, ironically predicting a remnant (Isaiah 37:4). Around the time of the Exile, we see more use of the term remnant to describe the hope that people will return to Jerusalem (Isaiah 10:22, 37:31,32; Zephaniah 2:7–10; Isaiah 11:11; Jeremiah 23:3; Ezekiel 14:22). The term comes finally to be used almost as a title for the post-exilic faith community (2 Chronicles 34:9; Haggai 1:14; Zechariah 8:6–8; Ezra 9:8). The psalms, in bearing witness to the hopeful element of remnant, translate that into defiance. The traditions will be preserved with a new focus, and that new focus is for a new kingdom.

Those who argue the case for a defiant "kingdom theology" nowadays (or at least as they did in the 1970s; you don't hear much about kingdom theology now) invariably point to the *prophets* of the Old Testament, especially Amos, Micah and the early part of the book of

Isaiah. Indeed, from the perspective of the prophets, as they look at society (presumably as God sees it), there is much material there to encourage a critical view of society and its leaders, its movers and shakers. They are critical of the various rulers of the day, and the decline, as they saw it, in the standards required by the Covenant. The Covenant set standards based on truth, justice, righteousness, mercy and love that the prophets used as a benchmark against which to judge society. Amos used the image of a plumbline to demonstrate that. Their message could well have been summed up in the slogan "We're better than this". However, there is probably more material in the *Psalms* than the prophets about the relationship between the state and the community of the faithful.

In the first place there are some psalms which look very much like *prophetic speeches/oracles* themselves. Psalm 50 is one example. It states its theme of God's judgement on society from the outset, making passing reference to the remnant:

> Our God comes and does not keep silent;
> before him is a devouring fire
> and a mighty tempest all around him.
> He calls to the heavens above
> and to the earth, that he may judge his people:
> "Gather to me my faithful ones,
> who made a covenant with me by sacrifice!"

> The heavens declare his righteousness,
> for God himself is judge.
>
> "Hear, O my people, and I will speak,
> O Israel, I will testify against you (Psalm 50:3–7).

The judgement that the psalmist sets out begins in terms reminiscent of Isaiah 58, which is read in many churches on Ash Wednesday. It's no use observing external rituals of religion and thinking that that is all religion demands:

> Is not this the fast that I choose:
> to loose the bonds of injustice,
> to undo the straps of the yoke,
> to let the oppressed go free,
> and to break every yoke?
> Is it not to share your bread with the hungry
> and bring the homeless poor into your house;
> when you see the naked, to cover them
> and not to hide yourself from your own kin?
> Then your light shall break forth like the dawn,
> and your healing shall spring up quickly;
> your vindicator shall go before you;
> the glory of the LORD shall be your rear guard.
> Then you shall call, and the LORD will answer;
> you shall cry for help, and he will say,
> "Here I am" (Isaiah 58:6–9).

God has no delight in the traditional sacrifices. Psalm 50 centres on the theme of sacrifices (understandable in a temple setting) and says that what counts is a *sacrifice of thanksgiving* (a phrase we use in most Eucharistic prayers today), and not some ritual that is offered in practical forgetfulness of God. It concludes:

> Mark this, then, you who forget God,
> or I will tear you apart, and there
> will be no one to deliver.
> Those who bring thanksgiving as their sacrifice
> honour me;
> to those who go the right way,
> I will show the salvation of God (Psalm 50:22,23).

This could have come straight out of a prophetic speech. Some people think the prophets did play a part in liturgy, sometimes to give a hopeful word at a time of despair; sometimes to give a word of judgement at a time of complacency. There are just a few psalms that look as if that might have happened, and such a prophetic interjection is sometimes used as an explanation of changes of tone in psalms such as Psalm 22. But that by no means exhausts the material which we might call political theology.

There is an awful lot in the Psalter about *kingship*. Scholarly debate about it has tended to be pastorally useless, concerned with obscure questions about exactly when ancient kings were crowned. We need to rediscover the sense that it is in these psalms that the post-exilic community defiantly counters political despair. Yes, we have to keep the stones—the words and ideas and visions of the prophets—but we keep them as an inspiration for a time that will come. Kingship and kingdom are terms that relate to government. As today, the policy of the government has practical implications in terms of its programme of lawmaking, distribution and use of tax monies, and administration of justice; and it also has a representative function. The government sets the tone for how other nations see us and the way we citizens see ourselves and our country's character (if you like). That is how the psalmists see the king. He represents Israel as much as he represents God in his governing and leading role. We want a government with which we can identify, a government that we can say stands for the values we regard as central to our character as a nation. Much of the Lineker debacle concerned exactly that. In the Old Testament, people had all these same feelings, but of necessity they were directed towards the king.

It is important to note that the Old Testament has a degree of ambiguity about the necessity for, and role of, the king. We see this clearly in 1 Samuel 8 and 9.

In 1 Samuel 8, people want a king not primarily because of the social chaos described in the book of Judges, as we might expect if we've been following the story. (There we find a recurring refrain: "In those days there was no king in Israel and everyone did what was right in their own eyes," e.g., Judges 17:6). That is *part* of the people's complaint when they come to Samuel to ask for a king. Samuel's sons Joel and Abiah were judges but they "did not follow in his ways but turned aside after gain; they took bribes and perverted justice (1 Samuel 8:3). No, the people want a king primarily to be like other nations (which is ironic), and to have a king "to lead us out to war and fight our battles" (1 Samuel 8:20, REB). In other words, the king will be judged by the people in terms of his victories and conquests.

God is unhappy at this development and so instructs Samuel to paint a negative picture of what having a king will entail (1 Samuel 8:11–18). God believes that *God* is their king. "They have not rejected you. It is I they have rejected" (1 Samuel 8:7). In Chapter 9, we see a different approach. God is there represented as being in favour of having a king, who will fight the Philistines, and he instructs Samuel to appoint Saul, and so Samuel anoints him and "God made him a different person" (1 Samuel 10:9, REB). It is these two different ideas of kingship that we see represented in the psalms. On the one hand, we have those psalms that celebrate the *kingship of God*. They appear mostly in the 90s as a group. These are sometimes called enthronement psalms, because they appear to have been written for a special liturgical occasion, possibly (I think) an annual occurrence, something like our Sunday after Ascension, or Sunday before Advent (Christ the King). Some people think this was a specific event, a coronation (God has *become* king rather than God *is* king; Psalm 97:1; 99:1, REB). I think there would have been more mention of anointing if that were the case. These are psalms:

- that are heavy with creation theology and creation hyperbole,
- that extol God as the chief god amongst many,
- that speak of the justice and covenant values that God represents and
- that describe God's kingship as extending widely geographically.

Some quotations from Psalm 96 will illustrate the point:

> Declare his glory among the nations,
> his marvellous works among all the peoples.
> For great is the LORD and greatly to be praised;
> he is to be revered above all gods.
> For all the gods of the peoples are
> idols (Psalm 96:3–5).

> Say among the nations, "The LORD is king!
> The world is firmly established; it
> shall never be moved.
> He will judge the peoples with equity."
> Let the heavens be glad, and let the earth rejoice;
> let the sea roar and all that fills it;
> let the field exult and everything in it.

> Then shall all the trees of the forest sing for joy
> before the LORD, for he is coming,
> for he is coming to judge the earth.
> He will judge the world with righteousness
> and the peoples with his truth (Psalm 96:10–13).

In fact, we have already mentioned this kind of psalm when we were talking about psalms that counter the despair of chaos. These are songs of defiance that say there is order, there is structure, there is destiny, a plan and an author. But they also exude a nationalistic optimism which to any external observer is rather like a league 2 lowly football team's supporters singing, "We're going to win the cup."

A brief history note here. David's kingdom of Israel contained all the "provinces" of the 12 tribes (each named after a son of Jacob). After his death, Solomon became king. For ordinary people, this was a disaster and seemed to fulfil the dire predictions of 1 Samuel 8 about the excesses of an earthly king. As we noted in Chapter 1, we see an ironic description of this in the account of the visit of the Queen of Sheba in 1 Kings 10. 1 Kings 11 describes Solomon turning away from YHWH towards the gods of his many concubines, as a result of which God decides to do away with him. After his death, representatives of the people come to King Rehoboam to ask that he be better than his father, but he takes the opposite course and, partly as a result, Israel is divided into two kingdoms. By far the bigger (11 tribes) was what became Samaria, the Northern kingdom, Israel. The tiny area around Jerusalem, Bethlehem and Hebron (Judah) was the area we know most about because that is where our scriptures largely originate. Judah (from where we get the term Jew) was a tiny speck of a place surrounded by great colonial nations such as Assyria, Egypt, Babylon, later Persia and Greece and Rome. It was totally insignificant in international terms, in terms of influence, but it stood on an important trade route and was therefore a worthwhile prize for empire builders.

That gives these songs of defiance a context and identifies them as political. And Judah didn't win the cup. From the sixth century BCE onwards, either its inhabitants were in exile or it was a client nation with a puppet administration during Bible times; it only became a nation again with internationally recognized borders (recognized since 1967 everywhere apart from Israel itself, according to UN Security Council resolution 242) in 1948. The enthronement psalms are like football anthems. They are theological statements of defiant hope against the odds and the evidence, and they are anthems we still sing, because we are still team God, Remnant United. The fundamental beliefs about the story of the world are beliefs to which we adhere. This place of justice, equity and righteousness is how we want the earth to be, and we aim to sing it and pray it into being. And we look at our own world and we say, "We're better than that."

The other kind of psalms are those which do not directly speak of the kingship of God, but rather of *God's appointed earthly ruler*, his anointed, his "messiah" (Psalm 2:7—quoted in Matthew 3:17; Luke 3:22; Mark 1:11 with reference to the New Testament Messiah, Jesus). These psalms are usually classified as "Royal Psalms", and they hardly feature in our Sunday worship at all. The only one on which hymns are based, so far as I can see, is Psalm 72, from which we get "Jesus shall reign where'er the sun" and "Hail to the Lord's anointed" (note how quickly we ascribe the sentiments to Jesus). The reason for that is, I think, related to the reason that the people wanted an earthly king in the first place. He was to lead them out in battle, and these psalms often appear very militaristic, dwelling on victories in battle:

> Blessed be the LORD, my rock,
> who trains my hands for war
> and my fingers for battle,
> my rock and my fortress,
> my stronghold and my deliverer,
> my shield, in whom I take refuge,
> who subdues the peoples under
> me (Psalm 144:1,2).

Nowadays we are uncomfortable singing this kind of thing. Editors of modern hymnbooks have begun to reflect this uneasiness by either changing the words of familiar hymns ("Onward Christian soldiers" becomes "Onward Christian pilgrims") or omitting them altogether (even when they are based on biblical passages, such as the Wesley hymn "Soldiers of Christ, arise").

But the Royal Psalms do have more to offer. They are not all battle-happy songs. Psalm 45 is a wedding poem, a love song, though even that mentions "gird on your sword at your side, you warrior king" (45:3), possibly just a note about correct dress. There are words for the king and for his bride—one of the gentlest of the Royal Psalms. But more than that, these psalms (leaving aside the militaristic language and imagery) do express a hope and vision for a better society than the one people see around them. They are songs of hopeful defiance in that sense. Psalm 144 expresses these hopes eloquently:

> May our sons in their youth
> be like plants full grown,
> our daughters like corner pillars,
> cut for the building of a palace.
> May our barns be filled
> with produce of every kind;
> may our sheep increase by thousands,
> by tens of thousands in our fields,
> and may our cattle be heavy with young.
> May there be no breach in the walls, no exile,
> and no cry of distress in our streets.

> Happy are the people to whom such blessings fall;
> happy are the people whose God is
> the LORD (Psalm 144:12–15).

These psalms are perhaps more important than we have usually given them credit for. They signal the beginning of the movement, described in the New Testament, from Israel as a *place*, to Israel as a *concept*. The kingdom is essentially the situation, wherever it may be, where God's reign is acknowledged and honoured. The sentiments of Psalm 144 could almost be thought of as the Old Testament equivalent of "The kingdom of heaven is like . . ." that we read in the New Testament parables of Jesus. It's an imagined and prayed-for future, again in defiance of the evidence all around them. It's not a million miles from our most frequently used prayer, "Thy kingdom come", our own longing for a society completely at one with the demands of the Covenant for mercy, justice, righteousness, truth and love. I think their prayer is not to be ignored. It mirrors our own, in the face of our own political despair.

We still sing a version of Psalm 103 in the hymn "Praise, my soul, the King of Heaven". If we were to read the statements of that psalm as intended descriptions of fact, we should rightly be suspicious:

> Bless the LORD, O my soul,
> and do not forget all his benefits—
> who forgives all your iniquity,

> who heals all your diseases,
> who redeems your life from the Pit,
> who crowns you with steadfast love and mercy,
> who satisfies you with good as long as you live
> so that your youth is renewed like the eagle's.
> The LORD works vindication
> and justice for all who are
> oppressed. (Psalm 103:2–6)

It is precisely the complaints that God does not seem to be doing these things that fill the psalms of lament. But the clue as to how to read the psalm properly comes at verse 19:

> The LORD has established his throne in the heavens,
> and his kingdom rules over all.

In other words, this is a description of what life is like *when* the kingdom of God is established. This is a prime example of an Old Testament, "The kingdom of God is like . . ."

The people who sing these psalms are not just looking forward to a new kingdom; they are also aware of their current predicament and their responsibility to "keep the stones", until that kingdom becomes a reality. These are the "stones" that tell of Israel's past. In particular, they tell of the liberating events of the Exodus, and they offer traditional reasoning about why the Exile happened. The post-exilic period sees thorough treatments of these themes in the theological histories provided, on the one hand, by writers who saw David as the last king who fulfilled his anointed role, and particularly kept the kingdom united. These writers saw human sin, provoking God's anger, as the reason for the Exile, and the biblical books from Joshua to 2 Kings, together with the prophecies of Jeremiah and his predecessors, Amos, Micah, Hosea and Zephaniah, set out their case. On the other hand, the history written as an alternative account in the books of Chronicles, Ezra and Nehemiah tell a similar story but with more of an eye to the institutions of Israel that will enable their continued existence as a people, after the Exile and the consequent Diaspora.

But this role of keeping and passing on the traditions is maintained at a popular level in liturgy also. That is probably a more effective way of doing so. Three psalms in particular are regarded as "historical" in this sense: Psalms 78, 105 and 106. Psalm 136 is added to this group by some scholars. Others prefer to regard it as a song of praise. Whatever we call it, it does recount the traditions but in a more formal liturgical fashion. This psalm is sometimes known as "the great Hallel", the great praise song, with its recurring refrain that God's love endures for ever. That is perhaps the most basic article of faith this community needs to live by.

Psalm 78 is essentially a condensed version of the first history mentioned above. It begins by stating its aim. The tradition is to be kept, remembered and passed on:

> Give ear, O my people, to my teaching;
> incline your ears to the words of my mouth.
> I will open my mouth in a parable;
> I will utter dark sayings from of old,
> things that we have heard and known,
> that our ancestors have told us.
> We will not hide them from their children;
> we will tell to the coming generation
> the glorious deeds of the LORD and his might
> and the wonders that he has done (Psalm 78:1–4).

The story it then goes on to tell is very much the "official" version of history. This is the story of a God who is generous beyond reproach and an ungrateful and sinful people that deserve all that is coming to them. God barely restrains himself but does so out of love for the people:

> They remembered that God was their rock,
> the Most High God their redeemer.
> But they flattered him with their mouths;
> they lied to him with their tongues.
> Their heart was not steadfast toward him;
> they were not true to his covenant.
> Yet he, being compassionate,
> forgave their iniquity
> and did not destroy them;
> often he restrained his anger
> and did not stir up all his wrath (Psalm 78:35–38).

But eventually God could take no more:

> He gave his people to the sword
> and vented his wrath on his heritage.
> Fire devoured their young men,
> and their young women had no marriage song.
> Their priests fell by the sword,
> and their widows made no
> lamentation (Psalm 78:62–64).

The psalm ends by invoking David as the ideal king:

> He chose his servant David
> and took him from the sheepfolds;
> from tending the nursing ewes he brought him
> to be the shepherd of his people Jacob,
> of Israel, his inheritance.
> With upright heart he tended them
> and guided them with skilful
> hand (Psalm 78:70–72).

Psalm 105 concentrates on the character of God rather than the sinfulness of humanity and is more reminiscent of the second history mentioned above. This story ends on a note of liberation, triumph and joy. For the people singing this psalm, it must have inspired faith in YHWH. Just as God gathered this scattered people once, he can do so again:

> So he brought his people out with joy,
> his chosen ones with singing.
> He gave them the lands of the nations,
> and they took possession of the
> wealth of the peoples,
> that they might keep his statutes
> and observe his laws.
> Praise the LORD! (Psalm 105:43–45).

Psalm 106 takes us back to the “official” version. It is headed in the NRSV Bible, “A Confession of Israel’s Sins”. But it locates the congregation who sings the psalm in a similar place to some congregations today, saying, in effect, “We didn’t deserve it, but you have redeemed us and will do so again”:

> Many times he delivered them,
> but they were rebellious in their purposes
> and were brought low through their iniquity.
> Nevertheless, he regarded their distress
> when he heard their cry.
> For their sake he remembered his covenant
> and showed compassion according to
> the abundance of his steadfast love.
> He caused them to be pitied
> by all who held them captive.
> Save us, O LORD our God,
> and gather us from among the nations,

> that we may give thanks to your holy name
> and glory in your praise (Psalm 106:43–47).

These are psalms we rarely use in church because they are rather long, and they seem to deal with national history in a way that does not concern us. But they do give us a further insight into the religious observance of a remnant community as "keepers of the stones", as well as those who "keep the rumour of God alive" in the present, who continue to hold a vision of a future kingdom, a future society which is true to the Covenant.

I have experienced churches that have this vocation today. I had a colleague once, an older and very wise man who said that he saw his ministry in terms of passing on the stories about the nature of God—stories like the Prodigal Son or the Good Samaritan—so that they would not disappear or be lost from the communal memory. During the Second World War, Dietrich Bonhoeffer described something similar as he felt the true Church was being overwhelmed by a nationalist, populist monster. In a famous letter of May 1944 to someone about to be baptized, he says this about the Church:

> It is not for us to prophesy the day (though the day will come) when men will once more be called to utter the word of God that the world will be changed and renewed by it. It will be a new language, perhaps quite non-religious,

> but liberating and redeeming—as was Jesus' language; it will shock people and yet overcome them by its power; it will be the language of a new righteousness and truth, proclaiming God's peace with men and the coming of his kingdom. . . . Till then the Christian cause will be a silent and hidden affair, but there will be those who pray and do right and wait for God's own time. May you be one of them (Bonhoeffer 1971, p. 102).

That is a modern example of "remnant ecclesiology".

The kingdom of God, the kingship of God, is the main theme of the first three Gospels, and their language is directly descended from the language we find in the Psalms. We no longer think of earthly monarchs as having a divine right to rule or as people directly appointed by God, even if we do anoint some of them with oil. Our hopefulness for a better kind of God-willed society became postponed to some future age among some New Testament religious groups, and we have inherited that, thinking of the kingdom of God as something in a future age, or after we're dead. Those who have tried to establish it in political real time have generally been disappointed and left cynical by the intervention of malign human intention. But the psalms can perhaps encourage us against cynicism and despair with their songs of defiant hope against the odds. It's a question for debate whether the world is improving or declining but, whatever our view, we must surely agree that a vision of a God-willed society is worth singing about—our responsibility is to make it a new song, and to keep the song alive.

Conversation with God

Sovereign God,
remnant is an unattractive word.
It conjures up pictures
of the last bit of carpet on the end of the
roll that won't fit anywhere;
the bit of cloth that's only good for a quilt.
The remains of the day.
And I've been in congregations that feel like that.
Old, once sprightly, once passionate, once radical,
wanting the world to be more like
the one they'd heard about and read the stories of.
Now resigned, nostalgic, tired.
"The same people do everything," they say,
"And we're not getting any younger."
The thing they loved, that gave shape to their lives,
they could not even persuade their children with,
and they have learned to live with that guilt.
It happened on our watch.
We are the remnant.
But we have hardly noticed that
you have a role for the remnant;

to keep the rumour of God alive and
to keep God on the world's agenda.
And not just any god,
but a God of mercy, truth and compassion;
a forgiving and redeeming God
with whom to worry governments
corrupt, careless, cavalier and, inevitably, collapsing.
And honestly,
holding the stories and living by their lessons
may be enough for now.
There will come a time when those
  stories are needed and sought.
So we pray the remnant prayer: your kingdom come,
and hope for a time
when our piece of cloth fit only for a quilt is just that,
the centrepiece of a new work of creative art:
a new truly Pentecostal quilt of
  many colours and designs,
diverse, welcoming and warm,
  attractive and desirable.

Yma o hyd. We are still here. Kindle in our
  remnant embers the fire of your love.

CHAPTER 6

We're marching to Zion

Hereford Cathedral in the UK is home to a very important map: a medieval treasure called the *Mappa Mundi* which is said to date back to around 1300. As its name suggests, it is a map of the world, but not quite as we know it. I think we might call it a map of a worldview, rather than a scientifically and geographically accurate map. Its most notable feature is that in the centre of the map we find the city of Jerusalem. That is what I mean by a worldview. Actually, all world maps perhaps unconsciously project a worldview. In some of those produced in Europe, Europe is large, out of proportion to its real place in the world. Maps from America give the impression that America is the only country in the world. And maps produced in New Zealand look altogether different from what we expect. People there wear T shirts saying "no longer down under" (that's the clue). All maps are really a mixture of history, geography and cultural awareness.

The *Mappa Mundi* is about the significance of places in relation to Jerusalem. We are used to maps that have north at the top but this one has east at the top. East is the direction of the rising sun, metaphorically the direction of resurrection and also the direction of Christ's expected parousia in tradition. The British Isles are at the bottom left. The map bears witness to the importance of Jerusalem throughout history, and especially to the cultures influenced by the great monotheistic religions of Judaism, Christianity and Islam. In the Old Testament, Jerusalem is revered as the city of David. It was captured by him from the Jebusites, who thought it impregnable (you'll capture this when you get rid of the blind and the lame, i.e., never). Capture it they did:

> David occupied the stronghold and named it the city of David. David built the city all around from the Millo inward (2 Samuel 5:9).

Later, Solomon built the first temple there, described in great detail in 1 Kings 7. That temple was destroyed at the time of the Exile, and when the exiles returned there was some discussion about how high a priority it was to rebuild it. Haggai 1 describes how YHWH took issue with the returnees. They thought that building a temple was something that could wait. God told them that they would never prosper until they made it a priority. Eventually it was rebuilt, and indeed the book of Psalms is sometimes called the hymnbook of the second temple. Exile had added the whole concept of what the Welsh call *hiraeth*, longing, to the idea of Jerusalem, and that is an idea that persists with the Jewish diaspora.

Mount Zion is the hilltop area of Jerusalem which David captured (about the size of a UK village), and Zion became the descriptive word for all that the temple and the palace represented in the identity of the people. Jerusalem is over 2,000 feet above sea level, and from every direction people have to go up to it. The Hebrew term *Aliah* (to ascend) still describes the longed-for journey to Jerusalem of modern Jews scattered throughout the world. Zion was reckoned as signifying the dwelling place of God. The ark of the Covenant containing the sacred tablets given to Moses on Mount Sinai was there. But Solomon's prayer of dedication makes clear the limits of that geographical location as the special location of God:

> But will God indeed dwell on the earth? Even heaven and the highest heaven cannot contain you, much less this house that I have built! Regard your servant's prayer and his plea, O LORD my God, heeding the cry and the prayer that your servant prays to you today; that your eyes may be open night and day toward this house, the place of which you said, "My name shall be there," that you may heed the prayer that your servant prays toward this place. Hear

> the plea of your servant and of your people Israel when they pray toward this place; O hear in heaven your dwelling place; hear and forgive (1 Kings 8:27–30).

According to Haggai, the temple is where God will reveal his glory. This significance extended, in Christian writing, to the realm of the hopes for a new age, a new earth and a new heaven as described first in the Old Testament prophets (Isaiah 25; Micah 4:1–3; Isaiah 2:2–4) and then in the New Testament book of Revelation. The new Jerusalem would be in the midst of the new earth as the *Mappa Mundi* portrays it, but now there would be no need for a new temple. Things had moved on. God simply dwelt in the midst of his people. But when psalms were written, the *place* was very important.

It is interesting to consider the importance of *place* in religious life. I think that importance has three elements, each of which conveniently begins with the letter H. The first is how a particular place comes to be objectively regarded as a *holy place*. In Genesis 28, Jacob had a dream whilst he was camping in the middle of nowhere, taking a rest on a long journey. The dream was sufficiently revelatory for Jacob to declare that God had been in the place, and he had not realized it. To mark the spot, he assembled a kind of primitive altar, and he gave the place a special name, Beth-el, meaning the house of God. From then on, places at which there has been a special revelation of God's presence have been revered, and often become the places that prompt pilgrimage; a kind of religious observance that is gaining in popularity in modern times.

Sometimes those revelations are in the form of a vision of the Virgin Mary, and sometimes the site of a recorded miracle. Holy places sometimes have an association with a particular saint. St Davids in Pembrokeshire is one such site I know well. In medieval times, two pilgrimages to St Davids were equivalent to one to Rome, and many modern pilgrims visit each year. The cathedral has responded with a renewed shrine and a pilgrimage education centre. Scenes of martyrdom, such as that of Thomas a Becket in Canterbury, have been centres of pilgrimage for centuries, as evidenced by Geoffrey Chaucer. In Israel/Palestine, holy sites abound, because they are places that Jesus visited, or are mentioned in the Gospels. Sometimes, as with Rome or Constantinople, Christian history has given them significance. Pilgrimage apart, there are places which have a recognized holiness by virtue of the activity with which they are presently associated, such as Taizé. In some places an ancient tradition has been repurposed, as in Iona. They are objectively certified.

Then there are places which have significance, reflected in our personal subjective religious life, because they represent a *homecoming*. They are places where we feel we specially belong, where we can be most properly ourselves. This understanding of place has a particular resonance with exiles, displaced people and refugees, for whom it has overtones of safety and refuge; and indeed, with anyone whose life and career has led them to many different places, who occasionally need to think about where they are from, and where they consider their true home to be.

Place is also an important element in *heritage*, when it is regarded as a key component of identity. David Goodhart's post-Brexit analysis of the result of the Referendum introduced the concept of dividing people into those "who see the world from Anywhere and the people who see it from Somewhere" (Goodhart 2017, p. 3). Anywheres are people who have travelled for education and career and they dominate our culture and society in Goodhart's view. "Such people have portable 'achieved' identities, based on educational and career success which makes them generally comfortable with new places and people." But alongside them are people who have not travelled far from their place of birth and whose identity is very much bound up with that place. "Somewheres are more rooted and usually have 'ascribed' identities—Scottish farmer . . . Cornish housewife." People who are motivated to search for their "roots" because of this sense of place are interested to find, if they do a DNA test, that part of their DNA derives from Scandinavia or South Africa. Place plays an important part in the lives of those who, having had a very varied life, seek in later years to impose a narrative on it, so that their lives are not just a sequence of unconnected events, but have a story. Each of these elements of place is important, and recognizable in the way that the psalms refer to Jerusalem.

Allied to a sense of place is a sense of *occasion*. It is one thing to visit religiously important places on your own, and sometimes it is more appropriate; but it is quite another to visit them in a company of like-minded people with a common purpose. They can then become lodged in the memory at a point where place and time intersect, as occasion.

The psalms that mention Jerusalem or, poetically, Zion, fall into several categories. There is one group of just six psalms that have long been recognized and categorized as "Songs of Zion" (46, 48, 76, 84, 87 and 122). Then there are four psalms that are clearly liturgical and for use at the temple in Jerusalem, which are sometimes called liturgical psalms. They are 15, 24, 68 and 134. Then there is a whole section of psalms, 120–134, that are called "Songs of Ascent", which are thought to have been a kind of pilgrim worship book for those attending the great festivals in Jerusalem, and they are preserved as a group. Finally, there are psalms which mention Jerusalem or Zion in passing, but which do not have it as a major theme, such as those that recount the history of Israel, mentioned in the last chapter.

We have already spoken of the people's need to establish a rock, a refuge, a place that defied chaos. The songs of Zion add a further dimension of security—peace/shalom, the Old Testament equivalent of what we now call wellness. Yes, these psalms describe all the fortifications and defences that make the place a refuge, but this is not the kind of fort from which troops go out to war; it is rather the dwelling of a God who executes judgement "to deliver all the afflicted in the land" (76:9). Psalm 122 is quite explicit. "Pray for the peace of Jerusalem . . . peace be within your ramparts and prosperity within your palaces. For the sake of these my brothers and friends I shall say, peace be within you. I shall pray for your wellbeing." Psalm 84 overflows with that sense of wellbeing:

> How lovely is your dwelling place,
>   O LORD of hosts!
> My soul longs, indeed it faints,
>   for the courts of the LORD;
>   my heart and my flesh sing for joy
>   to the living God.
> Even the sparrow finds a home
>   and the swallow a nest for herself,
>   where she may lay her young,
>   at your altars, O LORD of hosts,
>   my King and my God.
> Happy are those who live in your house,
>   ever singing your praise (Psalm 84:1–4).

This is a popular psalm for modern worship song writers, as we might imagine. The songs in this group are all popular, but that may be because the context in which they were sung is largely ignored.

Chapter 3 described how the psalms betray a certain sense of anxiety about the perceived absence of God. Zion stands, and Zion psalms stand, as a defiant rejoinder to that doubt. Despite Solomon's caveat, this is a place to go, a place to gather and a place to take part in liturgies that give a special sense of God's presence. I think we can understand that. It's partly why we revere churches nowadays. They are also places to gather, to celebrate in common defiance, to celebrate God's presence in his people, his word and his sacraments. And they too take on a life of their own: the place I went to Sunday school, the place I was confirmed, the place I was married and my parents are buried, and in between, the place where I have prayed and sung and perhaps wept and welcomed the space to reflect. A serious house on serious earth. Churches also become repositories of community memories through their plaques, registers and stained-glass windows.

Churches are important in remnant ecclesiology. Sometimes the decaying, uncared-for building symbolizes, for those who still attend, the state of the faith in modern society. In the 1960s, in Britain, many new "dual-purpose" churches were built, as the accompaniment to a new vision of the relationship between church and society. I have seen several church buildings in recent years that have repurposed existing, relatively ancient buildings. With the aid of grants, they have installed the latest green technology. Many community events take place in them, and a small space is usually reserved for the worshipping congregation and for funerals. Each of these styles of building says something about our idea of church, and the repurposed ancient church, technically fit for the future with its solar panels and digital connectivity, is a positive remnant expression. They can continue to be effective, perhaps more effective, repositories of community history.

We see that in the Psalms too. There are those psalms which, as we have seen, mean little to us because they are usually long and do not speak to our own sense of identity. These historical psalms tell the story of the people and confirm in them a sense of shared identity. They include the so-called "great Hallel" of Psalm 136. Hallel psalms contain the refrain Halleluia (may Yahweh's name be praised), and there is one group of them, 113–118. These psalms characteristically recount Israel's official history, but in a context of gratitude for maintaining them. "It is good to give thanks to the Lord, for his love endures for ever" is a constant refrain (in 136, or here in verse 1 of 106). That psalm goes on for a further 47 verses and concludes, "Blessed be the LORD the God of Israel, from everlasting to everlasting. Let all the people say Amen." (This is who we are.)

We can see the importance of these psalms for a community unsure of its identity. Before the Exile everything was much simpler. God was the God of Israel. Other people could have other gods that were nothing like as effective as the God of Israel, but this God had singled out Israel to be a Covenant partner, and this was part of the nation's specialness, small as it was:

> Happy is the nation whose God is the LORD,
> the people whom he has chosen as
> his heritage (Psalm 33:12).

But once the realization grew that there was but one God, it was easy for the particularity of Israel to be forgotten or disregarded. (Christians today often ask why we should bother with the Old Testament at all.) God's concern was the whole world, the whole of creation indeed, and the whole of history. What place did Israel's history have to play, and what did that mean for its present relationship with God? These were questions made even more acute with the advent of Christianity which, in Paul's writings at least, wanted to assume that Christianity was the new Israel (Galatians 6:16). What then of the old Israel?

The *liturgical psalms* have in common a use that would be difficult to imagine outside a liturgical occasion. Psalm 134, which is set in the Anglican service of Compline, is a short psalm that notes the priests who minister "night after night". In other words, it speaks of a usage not unlike that of Compline. There is something reassuring about the psalm which speaks of the regularity of the temple, and its persistence and reliability. It does not cease to function when pilgrims go home. In the relatively recent past, Anglican priests were enjoined to say the offices of Morning and Evening Prayer in their churches daily, after ringing the bell. The point of the bell was that people who could not attend and who were going about their daily business could be assured that the liturgical life of the church continued on their behalf. Something similar is suggested here.

Psalms 24 and 15 are mostly concerned with the fitness of people to enter the temple. This is not just a tourist destination as many people might see modern cathedrals but rather a serious physical symbol of the Covenant, peculiar to Israel, between the nation and God. Therefore, access should be restricted to those who honour the Covenant by living a blameless life and not lending money on interest (!) in the case of Psalm 15, or to one with clean hands and a pure heart in the case of Psalm 24. This latter psalm has the responsorial form which presumably preceded and enabled access. These two psalms speak to the particularity of the Covenant community.

Perhaps the most interesting is Psalm 68. This contains many of the important religious aspects of place. There is the detailed description of the religious occasion:

> Your solemn processions are seen, O God,
> the processions of my God, my
> King, into the sanctuary—

the singers in front, the musicians last,
between them young women
playing tambourines:
"Bless God in the great congregation,
the LORD, O you who are of Israel's fountain!"
There is Benjamin, the least of them, in the lead,
the princes of Judah in a body,
the princes of Zebulun, the princes
of Naphtali (Psalm 68:24–27).

Exodus, Covenant values and Exile are referenced:

Father of orphans and protector of widows
is God in his holy habitation.
God gives the desolate a home to live in;
he leads out the prisoners to prosperity,
but the rebellious live in a parched land.
O God, when you went out before your people,
when you marched through the wilderness,
the earth quaked, the heavens poured down rain
at the presence of God, the God of Sinai,
at the presence of God, the God
of Israel (Psalm 68:5–8).

And there is some attempt to combine the universal God and the God of Israel:

Sing to God, O kingdoms of the earth;
sing praises to the Lord,

O rider in the heavens, the ancient heavens;
listen, he sends out his voice, his mighty voice.
Ascribe power to God,
whose majesty is over Israel
and whose power is in the skies.
Awesome is God in his sanctuary,
the God of Israel;
he gives power and strength to his people.
Blessed be God! (Psalm 68:32–35).

This was obviously a well-known psalm, as it is quoted in the New Testament (Ephesians 4:8).

The people's desire for security in an insecure world was not just limited to contexts of earthquakes, or wars, or other *extraordinary* things. It was a desire for a period of social stability in the face of anarchy. The psalms are interested in how that is to be achieved and their answer is to keep God's law and adhere to the Covenant. Several psalms make reference to the Torah. It is notable perhaps that the book begins with one of those. Psalm 1 is a psalm commending the Torah. This is the way to a godly life, a life that is as perfect as can be. Psalm 119 is a cleverly worked acrostic which takes the A to Z equivalent of the Hebrew language, and begins each section of the psalm with the letters in order. (In the first section all the lines begin with *aleph*, the second with *beth*, the third with *gimel*, and so on.) There are 22 letters in the Hebrew alphabet, hence 22 sections in the psalm: a literary version of perfection. The subject is

Torah, and the psalm, in its completeness, demonstrates the Torah's perfection. There is both social security and national identity at play here. Not limited to any one place, the obvious place to celebrate Torah would be Jerusalem.

The songs of ascent are a mixed bunch. They are 120–134 and include laments, a penitential psalm and psalms which declare trust, such as Psalm 121. Psalm 125 sums up: "Those who trust in the Lord are like Mount Zion. It cannot be shaken, it stands fast for ever." All these pilgrim songs are short—the sort of thing you might sing or recite whilst pausing on a journey. Some psalms in this group are reflective, as you would expect. I have always loved the quiet simplicity of Psalm 131:

> O LORD, my heart is not lifted up; (proud)
>   my eyes are not raised too high; (haughty)
> I do not occupy myself with things
>   too great and too marvellous (difficult) for me.
> But I have calmed and quieted my soul,
>   like a weaned child with its mother;
>   my soul is like the weaned child that is with me.
> O Israel, hope in the LORD
>   from this time on and forevermore.

The whole theme of pilgrimage is too big for us to consider in any detail now, but it is a persistent theme, and one which combines seriousness and destination with congregation and journey, and which keeps hope alive. But—and this is the point—the hope, the optimism was at odds with the experience of those post-exilic people singing these psalms. Because, in 597 BCE, it all came crashing down. Psalm 74 recounts how the temple was sacked and desecrated by the invading Babylonians:

> Your foes have roared within your holy place;
> they set up their emblems there.
> At the upper entrance they hacked
> the wooden trellis with axes.
> And then, with hatchets and hammers,
> they smashed all its carved work.
> They set your sanctuary on fire;
> they desecrated the dwelling place of your name,
> bringing it to the ground.
> They said to themselves, "We will utterly subdue
> them";
> they burned all the meeting places of
> God in the land (Psalm 74:4–8).

Bearing in mind the importance of this special place in the religious landscape of the people, we can begin to see the utter hopelessness that this caused. It wasn't just the loss of an ancient building. The people's heart had been wrenched out:

> O God, why do you cast us off forever?
> Why does your anger smoke against
> the sheep of your pasture?

> Remember your congregation, which you acquired
> long ago,
> which you redeemed to be the tribe of your
> heritage.
> Remember Mount Zion, where you
> came to dwell (Psalm 74:1,2).
>
> We do not see our emblems;
> there is no longer any prophet,
> and there is no one among us
> who knows how long.
> How long, O God, is the foe to scoff?
> Is the enemy to revile your name
> forever? (Psalm 74:9,10).

Jerusalem was the bulwark, the refuge, the strong tower that defiantly stood against the scoffers and enemies. It was the evidence of God's presence. Now everything was lost. It is as well to remember that this psalm is in a collection that also speaks of the glories of Zion, and in an Old Testament that invests much in Zion. John Newton's hymn "Glorious things of thee are spoken" is actually based on Isaiah 33:20, but its sentiments are echoed in the Psalms. The picture we should have in our mind as we sing those psalms is of a people returned from Exile to a ruined city, yearning for the greatness it once represented, and the presence of God it once guaranteed.

The most famous reflection on the experience of the subsequent Exile is found in Psalm 137, and it is no surprise that Zion is its theme:

> By the rivers of Babylon—
> there we sat down, and there we wept
> when we remembered Zion.
> On the willows there
> we hung up our harps.
> For there our captors
> asked us for songs,
> and our tormentors asked for mirth, saying,
> Sing us one of the songs of Zion! (Psalm 137:1–3).

The sheer poignancy of this psalm has meant that it has resonance for modern exiles and has been recorded by modern bands and artists such as Boney M and Don MacLean.

Perhaps we all have our Zions. I remember doing a TV documentary about life in the churches in Newport, Gwent, entitled *Is the Church on its Knees?* One huge Baptist chapel in the middle of the town was now derelict and condemned, but we managed to find a family who had once worshipped there. They had pictures of Sunday school trips and Passion plays and crowds of people for the Gymanfaoedd Ganu (singing festivals). I can still remember the wistful, almost tearful, look of the oldest lady in the family. "We thought it would never end," she said. Of course it is wrong to invest all our religious capital in a building, and that is a mistake some make. But when we lose a place that has special significance in our lives, for our identity and for our religious security, and we continue in the faith despite everything, in faithful defiance, then we are close to the experience of the psalmist. The writer of Psalm 74 praises God despite everything. He recalls the axioms of his faith. He lives in faithful incomprehension and honest sadness. Perhaps we can recall and appreciate afresh the sentiments of Psalm 31:21:

> Blessed be the Lord!
> For he has shown me the wonders
> of his love in a besieged city.

Psalms remind us of what defiant faith looks like; faith that refuses to give in to meaninglessness or tragedy. Faith that continues to find value in liturgy, gathering, pilgrimage and prayer; that declares the presence of God against the odds. In the Psalms, these feelings find a focus in Zion. I think we all perhaps have our special places, our places of identity and significance, our places of memory and longing, our places for reflection and where prayer seems particularly appropriate. But those acts of defiant faith are always in tension with the lived experience of grief and despair. And we can take heart from the fact that this book of Psalms was assembled by those who returned from Exile with their football anthem-like defiance and their refusal to stop singing. We are still here.

We are now in a better position to review the concerns, listed in the Introduction, that prompted the book in the first place. Key amongst them is the charge that scholarship has presented us with a commentary on the Psalms that is pastorally useless. It was suggested that this is largely connected with ignoring their context-in-use. Since the last quarter of the twentieth century, Old Testament scholarship has taken a radically new direction. Before then, the Old Testament was thought to be largely about the Exodus and works on the Pentateuch or Hexateuch predominated. Since that time, there has been a new emphasis on the effects of the Exile, and a consensus has emerged that the Old Testament tells a story about the Exodus in response to the experience of Exile. The Old Testament (or its Hebrew equivalent) is a post-exilic enterprise. Scholars vary as to how old the traditions are that go to make it up, but they agree that the editorial process was a post-exilic one, determined to some extent by the trauma that people had experienced.

This trauma was not just the obvious physical one, but rather the crisis of faith that the Exile triggered. The people of Israel had been promised a land, progeny and a special relationship with God; the Exile seemed to negate all three. The choices that confronted people then were either to abandon faith (or transfer it to some other supposed deity), or to continue in faith on the basis that there was more to God than they had imagined, and that the Exile was in some sense a new revelation of God. This sense should be recognizable for Christians. Our faith began where it ought, on any rational grounds, to have ended. The one believed to be (son of) God had been crucified. Disappointment and disillusion should have extinguished any further hope. But those who continued in faith did so on the basis that this was meant to teach us something new about God, and that our understanding of God hitherto had been at best incomplete.

Scholars have brought the study of the Old Testament to life by reading it in a way that *is* pastorally useful, in terms of responses to trauma, which is a universal interest. A good example is Walter Brueggemann's *Cadences of Home* (Brueggemann 1997), which lists sections of the Old Testament as resources for returning exiles. Unfortunately, Psalms has been neglected in this project, and that is surely odd. The same editorial process that brought about the great Old Testament histories, collected the sayings of the prophets, and placed them in a narrative, was employed, at about the same time, to give the faithful their hymnbook of the second temple. Psalms and songs from over the centuries were brought together to provide the ultimate resource in the face of the theological maelstrom and physical hardships of the post-exilic period; yet those psalms still had a universal outlook in giving voice to the concerns that are common to humanity.

The fact of the Psalms being hidden in plain sight does not, I think, need to be argued, but a further aim was to try to hear the voice of ordinary theology, ordinary religion. The proposal was that it should be possible to hear that voice, rather than the "official" line in the Psalms, and so it has proved. Ordinary theologians do not recognize themselves as such. They are more likely to identify with Psalm 131: "I do not occupy myself with great matters, or with things that are too hard for me. But I still my soul and make it quiet, like a child upon its mother's breast my soul is quieted within me" (Psalm 131:2,3, CCP). The voice of ordinary religion is sometimes argumentative, sometimes subversive and yet it is defiantly faithful. It is a voice with which many will identify nowadays.

And so, what is the future of psalmody in our liturgy and devotion? Will the psalms continue to be cut and pasted to appear as the happy songs for people whose whole life is centred on religion? Or will they find a new place as reflections of ordinary theology sung by those thoroughly engaged with a broken and suffering world, but who want to point defiantly to its glimpses of joy, of peace, of justice, of mercy, of generosity and love: those who have indeed recognized the wonders of God's love in a besieged city?

Conversation with God

God of all our Zions
I remember listening to the Beatles' first
serious song (as it has been called),
"In my life".
It began, "There are places I remember all
my life, though some have changed."
And it went on to link those places with
"lovers and friends I still can recall".
And when I hear it now—I've kept a record—
it makes me think about my life and my places,
and how my places are connected
with lovers and friends,
and how my memories combine places and people,
and how they've helped to make me who I think I am.

If I were a racehorse,
they'd describe me as
by Harold, out of Edith
and part of where I'm from, and who I am
is surely contained there.
But places, lovers and friends also have their part
in the tangle.

Bishop John Robinson
when asked about the influences in his life
said, "Certain books and the men to
whom they meant much."

For me, it would be
certain people and the places where I met them.
But it's more than that.
It's why we were there and
what we were doing
and the things we think we achieved
and what it was teaching me;
and it's about the regrets as well as the joys.

The question that the psalmist asks,
what is man that thou art mindful of him?
is prompted by the vastness of creation,
and the search for a fixed point within it.

But I ask that question, as well,
because of the vastness of history
in which I am equally insignificant.
Places help me to put an order, frame a narrative.
The chapters of my life would each have place names.

I suppose I am an Anywhere,
but that does not mean
that everywhere is equally significant.
I too have my Zions:
very special places
foundation places
where you, God, were especially real and
   where prayer was especially vital.
They are inevitably connected with lovers and friends.

And visiting reminds me and
brings it all back.

My first parish as Vicar,
a living as they call it,
was one such place.
Full of life in all its variety.
A wonderful vibrant place full of voices and pictures
and pilgrims
that I still recall.
And now that church is empty,
for sale,
and I feel its loss
deeply.
It's as if part of me has been denied,
written out of history.

For me, it is still a holy place in all
  its decay and brokenness
and the graveyard is full of those who brought it to life.
Their monuments there
are their defiance.

And glorious things of thee, yes Thee,
are spoken by those
who live and love and remember and tell.

Afterthought

I began by asking you to imagine that we were compilers of a worship book for use in the second temple in Jerusalem sometime after the Exile, probably around the third century BCE. Our study has helped to define the context in which we were working. It appears that worshippers felt themselves within a polarized society in which the old certainties of public religion could no longer be taken for granted. There are hints of this in Haggai 1:2–11. The returning exiles were facing a devastated city and country and their first instinct was not to rebuild a church. But the prophets told them they would not prosper until that was made a priority. We can only imagine public feeling about seeing resources going into the building of the temple (the temple they had already thought to be a secondary priority) when they themselves were starving and barely subsisting (Haggai 1:6). Antagonism toward the community of faith is well documented throughout Psalms, in the form of the enemies, adversaries, mockers and scoffers. Things could hardly have improved with the edict that all foreign wives should be dismissed (Ezra 10).

Imagine yourself in a settled family group only to have the authorities tell you that your wives and your own children should be banished. Although there is no mention of women with foreign husbands, presumably the same would have happened to them. The careful administrative details recorded make the whole process even more sinister. Your name's on a list.

As compilers we have done a fantastic job in these circumstances. We have made sufficient reference to the landmarks of meaning and identity in our traditional history to satisfy the ultra-nationalists, whilst showing tremendous empathy, as we allow those who are suffering to have a voice and a context in which to address God directly. The initial emphasis on lament has set a context from which the whole variety of psalms included can be understood. We have provided, probably unwittingly, a record of how a remnant community, albeit a pre-Christian one, can understand its religious observance and theology. From our modern perspective, we may be able to see points of similarity. Christians in the West generally, and the UK in particular for our purposes, can often feel like a remnant community themselves. The Psalms may help us to develop our own worship patterns and religious life, and give us food for reflection about our own relationships, both with God and with our society.

If we ask the simple question, what did ordinary people want from religion, we are now in a position to make an initial and tentative list. They needed *a place to lament*. They needed a place to articulate their plight, to put their case, and to tell their story. This was their only medium. They had no public media, no social media. They could not publicly articulate their plight in drama or art. Lament to God was a real contribution to what we would now call their mental health. They sought a *refuge*. They needed fixed points. They wanted something or someone that was reliable, reassuring and dependable, which would help them make sense of the changes and chances of this fleeting life. They needed the fixed points to maintain a belief that life was not a series of accidents; that it had structure, purpose and destiny, through which their experience could be interpreted. And they needed *a liturgical path*, a liturgical process that would lead them from despair to hope; from grief and lament to joy and celebration.

The key figure is of course God. They look to *God as one who hears prayer*, who is interested in me, who cares about me, and with whom I can be familiar to a degree. When I look at the prayers in the Psalms, I am more struck by the need to speak and the need to be heard than I am by the need to have the answer I have arrived at for my problem. God can be trusted, once I am sure he has heard. I am reminded of a time when I was a TA Chaplain on an exercise in Germany where we were at war with "orange forces". As Chaplain I had a degree of freedom of movement denied to others, and I recall visiting one soldier in charge of a radar truck, who had been stuck in a field on his own for several days. We had the wide-ranging kind of conversation one has with a person who has had no chance to speak for a while. He had done a lot of thinking in that time, particularly about his home situation and closest relationships. He had put his thoughts in a letter and, as I left, he asked me to post it to his wife. I said that I might not be able to do so because we were forbidden from going into German shops (we were at war and orange forces were everywhere), and I had no stamp. He said that it didn't matter. The important thing for him was that he had written it and sent it. Some people think prayer is like that. But the psalmists definitely wanted to be heard.

Moral chaos is also feared, and the psalms give reassurance that God is a God of justice and, more than that, God is a *guarantor of justice.* The general picture that emerges is that they see God as judge, but they expect that God will judge them to be innocent and their opponents to be guilty. The evidence of the Covenant, and the Torah which results from it, are important enough for the Torah to be the subject of the very first psalm. The picture of God that the psalms encourage is more nuanced than the phrase "Old Testament God of Justice" usually conjures up. The character of God is in a sense revealed in the Torah and the Covenant, but that does not make God an unfeeling legalist, and one to be greatly feared. Judges nowadays are far less fearsome than in Bible times, when they had powers of life and death. I once had a judge parishioner who was related to the "hanging judge Jeffreys" of medieval England. I used to take him communion in his final days, and he took delight in showing me the black cap he used to wear when sentencing people to death. I was glad to be between him and the door.

The psalms show us a God who affirms our humanness, and is pleased with how creation has worked out. *God forgives and redeems where necessary*, but personal sin is not the overriding theme of religion it has sometimes been in Christian history. Too often, the psalms have been read as though it were. Eli Jenkins' Prayer in *Under Milk Wood* by Dylan Thomas might sum up the predominant ambience of the psalms.

> We are not wholly bad or good
> Who live our lives under Milk Wood;
> And Thou I know wilt be the first
> To see our best side, not our worst.

The relationship to wider creation inspires awe and wonder, and the relationship of God to the "social" world as well as the physical one is emphasized. Religion *offers a way to be a critical friend to society*, thoroughly engaged with the political process. Above all, the temple itself provides a place and a structure where individuals and the whole community of faith can articulate all of this: *a place where God makes his name to dwell.*

Perhaps these categories give us material for reflection today. In our remnant state, confused by much, despairing of much, and having to put Jesus into the mix, I wonder have we asked too much of God, or expected too little.

Bibliography

Bonhoeffer, Dietrich, *Letters and Papers from Prison*, enlarged edn, ed. and tr. Eberhard Bethge (London: SCM Press, 1971).

Brueggemann, Walter, *The Message of the Psalms: A Theological Commentary* (Minneapolis, MI: Augsburg Press, 1984).

Brueggemann, Walter, *Cadences of Home: Preaching Among Exiles* (Louisville, KY: Westminster John Knox Press, 1997).

Brueggemann, Walter, *From Whom No Secrets Are Hid* (Louisville, KY: Westminster John Knox Press, 2014).

Gillingham, Susan, *Psalms Through the Centuries: Volume One* (Chichester: Wiley-Blackwell, 2012).

Goodhart, David, *The Road to Somewhere: The Populist Revolt and the Future of Politics* (London: Hurst, 2017).

Pleins, J. David, *The Psalms: Songs of Tragedy, Hope, and Justice* (Maryknoll, NY: Orbis Books, 1993).

Sölle, Dorothee, *Suffering* (Philadelphia: Fortress Press, 1975).

Sweet, J. P. M., *Revelation* (London: SCM Press, 1979).

Westermann, Claus, *Praise and Lament in the Psalms* (Atlanta, GA: John Knox Press, 1981).

Zimmerli, Walther, *Old Testament Theology in Outline*, tr. David E. Green (Edinburgh: T&T Clark, 1978).

Acknowledgements

I first shared the idea for this work with the Liverpool Cathedral Postgraduate Learning Community, and I am grateful to them for that invitation and their continuing interest. As a result, I designed a Lent Course which was delivered at my home cathedral of St Paul, Nicosia, in 2023. This book has grown from that course, and I am also grateful for the responses to the course which helped me to shape it. My friend Leslie Francis has acted as a critical friend throughout its development, and I consider myself fortunate in that critical friendship. The encouragement I have had from my editor Dr Natalie Watson has been crucial. From our first conversations in Cyprus to the present finished publication, her enthusiasm and editorial care have been my companion and I am thankful.

Milton Keynes UK
Ingram Content Group UK Ltd.
UKHW022013131123
432501UK00010B/270